Creative ICT
in the Classroom

Using new tools for learning

GW00725422

**The Learning Discovery
Centre Team**

Published by
Network Continuum Education
PO Box 635, Stafford, ST16 1BF

www.networkcontinuum.co.uk
www.continuumbooks.com

An imprint of the Continuum International Publishing Group Ltd

First published 2006
© The Learning Discovery Centre Team 2006

ISBN-13: 978 1 85539 207 6
ISBN-10:   1 85539 207 0

The right of the Learning Discovery Centre Team (Kudsia Batool, Cheryl Eyre, Adrian Horner, Bill How and Guy Shearer) to be identified as the authors of this work has been asserted in accordance with Sections 77 and 78 of the Copyright, Designs and Patents Act 1988.

Every effort has been made to contact the copyright holders of materials reproduced in this book. The publishers apologize for any omissions and will be pleased to rectify them at the earliest opportunity.

Managing editor: Melanie Gray
Layout by: Marc Maynard, Network Continuum Education
Cover design by: Neil Hawkins, Network Continuum Education
Illustrations by: Katherine Baxter

Printed in Great Britain by MGP Books Ltd, Bodmin, Cornwall

Contents

Foreword

This book contains many practical ways of working towards the creative classroom and locates the use of ICT as a set of resources to take with us on the journey. It's important we continue to search out new ways of using the tools of our time – the classroom and this book take the search forward.

It may be possible, if we were to trust ourselves, to build a whole curriculum around telling stories and making things. The authors of this book have stepped beyond the refuge of general and generic advice to describe specific tried-and-tested projects. By reinvigorating the potential use of classroom perennials and familiar software such as PowerPoint, they are also taking us forward from familiar ground.

The focus of *Creative ICT in the Classroom* is on active and exploratory learning opportunities. It details the potential available if children take an active role as constructors of their own knowledge assisted by a variety of media tools. By describing how to use models and toys in creative play, we are reminded of the potential unleashed when we occupy the hand and free the mind.

Guidance on how to use sound recordings and students' soundtracks is particularly welcome in an age that seems easily distracted by the moving image. It is possible to forget that sound often carries most of the meaning in media communications, and this book reminds us of its power in the hands of learners. Elsewhere, the use of GPRS and portable phone-based technologies hint at how we can utilize these commercial tools for powerful learning.

Teachers, assistants and others charged with 'passing on knowledge' have, from the earliest times, looked to the wax tablet, the slate and, more recently, the overhead projector and the laptop. The author James Flint observes that it is our technology that defines us: 'We are our technology. Human beings weren't worthy of the name until they had come up with the axe, the loin cloth and the pot.' In *Creative ICT in the Classroom*, the 'slate' rides again as a Tablet PC, where practical uses of unique journal-writing software abound. The motivational effects of robotics and competitive play are also well rehearsed, as is the use of adventure and investigative role play. The digital tools are never suggested or deployed just for the sake of it; they are used because they allow the activity to rise and soar beyond what is otherwise possible. The need for collaboration is made powerfully to ensure the opportunities are less about 'me, me, me' and more to do with 'us, us, us'.

As you digest the guidance in this book, remember that the final arbiters of the opportunity will be you – the classroom teacher or assistant. Enjoy the journey and let the practical advice and inspirational ideas serve as trusted and friendly signposts.

John Davitt
Author of *New Tools for Learning: Accelerated learning meets ICT* (2005)

About the authors

Kudsia Batool

Kudsia is one of the five e-learning consultants who make up the Learning Discovery Centre team working to transform teaching and learning in Northamptonshire, to encourage innovation and creativity, and to raise standards. Kudsia believes we should use ICT as a tool to help us achieve this but that innovation is about more than technology – it's about a change in thinking and a change in practice. She has worked as a teacher, a broadband development consultant and sometime university lecturer. Kudsia is passionate about movie making and using ICT for strange and unusual educational activities that make people say 'Wow!'.

Cheryl Eyre

Cheryl is an e-learning consultant at the Learning Discovery Centre. She has taught pupils from Key Stages 1 to 5 in performing arts and humanities, mainly in the UK but also in France, Germany and Austria. Her specialist subject is music, particularly music technology. She also has experience of mentoring teachers, tutoring for the Open University and working within the television and film industry.

Adrian Horner

Adrian has been an e-learning consultant at the Learning Discovery Centre for over two years. Beginning his teaching career at the same time the National Curriculum was set up, he taught in several primary schools for 15 years before moving into advisory work. Working within two local authorities to support schools in their use of ICT has given Adrian a wide experience of the range of ICT taught in primary schools. His enthusiasms are around the creative use of ICT to stimulate learning. In particular, he has a keen interest in using Lego and computer control to develop aspects of learning.

Bill How

Bill began his career in automotive engineering and started teaching part-time on adult education courses in 1987. He has also spent time working in vocational training (training body and paint apprentices for Lotus Cars) before joining further education as a lecturer in 1991, specializing in engineering and staff development.

In addition to teaching, Bill was an awarding body external verifier, moderator and marking examiner for a number of years, helping to develop the question bank that eventually became the first vocational online testing system.

As one of the original Becta Information Learning Technology (ILT) champions, Bill was seconded part-time to the Learning and Skills Development Agency as a regional e-learning support co-ordinator and then full-time to the National Information and Learning Technology Association (NILTA) as a national manager responsible for co-ordinating regional activities. In his NILTA role, Bill was responsible for operating NILTA's event programme relating to the DfES e-Learning Strategy consultation and for rolling out NILTA's part in the National Learning Network Adult and Community Learning initiative.

Bill firmly believes in the concept of lifelong learning and the importance of using pedagogic strategies that develop a learner's adragogic (adult or independent) skills and strategies. Using ICT as a tool for valuing the learner's preferred devices to help achieve and develop independent learning is key to the Learning Discovery Centre projects and themes he has developed to date, including ICT Lite, code breaker and e-me – a personal online evidence repository.

Guy Shearer

Guy trained as a physicist and worked briefly as an engineer before training to be a teacher. He has worked in a variety of schools since 1987, including 11 to 16 comprehensives, community colleges and international schools, as a teacher of a range of subjects, a head of department and a deputy headteacher.

Since 2003, Guy has worked for Northamptonshire County Council, leading the development of the Learning Discovery Centre – a leading-edge venue for learning with a team of consultants committed to working across the education sector on improvement through change (as opposed to improvement through just working harder). Guy and the team are passionate about real classroom change being something you have to feel as well as know.

He has presented and run workshops in the UK and overseas on a number of ICT-related themes, the common thread always being the search for simplicity and the desire to escape from technology making teaching and learning ever more complex and difficult.

Authors' acknowledgements

The ideas in this book were inspired, tried out on and knocked into shape by the teachers and children of Northamptonshire schools and colleagues from a host of agencies with whom we have been lucky enough to work since we began in 2003. Our sincere thanks to all the people who have directly or indirectly contributed to our work.

Introduction

It seems to be a generally accepted wisdom that creativity in learning is a good thing. This means different things to different people; perhaps 'learning to be creative' for the new information age, or 'learning through creativity' to raise standards.

It also seems to be accepted that ICT is a pretty good thing and, again, we have more than one possible interpretation; is it learning about ICT through using it, or learning better as a result of ICT use?

What creativity and ICT have in common is that for many learners they continue to be extras. We do 'proper learning' most of the time and, as a special treat, we get to do creative projects or work in the computer room.

The creative classroom is a place where creativity and the use of ICT are integral parts of 'proper learning', and that is what this book is all about.

How to use this book

Each chapter in this book describes self-contained projects that you could adapt to your own setting. For most projects we have tried to avoid referring to specialist software or other tools that involve spending lots of money, but there are areas, such as in Chapter 6, where we have had to refer to specific software. In general, we have used and referred to Microsoft Office-type software (for which there are free alternatives that also work well) and almost all the products we mention are free.

Read through the whole chapter as we have tried to introduce how the ideas for the project might fit into your classroom in the first part, and then give you the tools to do it yourself in the second.

To help you get the most out of this book, we have used the following features:

WEBSITE ➡ Links to relevant **websites** are indicated in the margin.

CD-ROM ➡ You will also find links to the **CD-ROM** in the margin whenever there is a file or a hyperlink either to show you what we mean through examples or to direct you to where you can find a useful resource or read further.

 ➡ **Tools** boxes show some of the equipment and software you might use for your own projects. The lists are not exhaustive by any means – simply a pointer if you need ideas on what to use.

 ➡ **Key points** boxes highlight the main ideas involved in the project.

Top tips ➡ **Top tips** boxes give hints and tips to get the most out of the ideas in the chapter.

 ➡ **ICT Lite** boxes offer suggested alternatives to more traditional approaches. ICT doesn't always mean using PCs – indeed you can often have better learning when you keep it simple.

We have endeavoured to ensure that the website addresses in this book and on the CD-ROM are correct and active at the time of going to press. However, we cannot guarantee that a site will remain live or that the content is or will remain appropriate.

There are several books – many available from Network Continuum Education – that can give you a good grounding in thinking about learning. Therefore, we have made the assumption that you are an enlightened learner and don't need further explanation of visual, auditory or kinesthetic (VAK) learning. For more information, we suggest you read *New Tools for Learning* by John Davitt (Network Continuum Education, 2005) if you find yourself in unfamiliar territory.

A journey not a destination

Learning isn't a place we are going to. The creative classroom isn't an objective that can ever be achieved. The value is in the learning that happens along the way. Whether or not your learners or you feel creative, whether or not they consider how to use ICT – these considerations don't matter. What matters is that we are working to expose learners to a richer diet of ideas and experiences every time they step into our teaching space.

Chapter 1

Story-telling

Telling a story is one of the most basic, enjoyable and creative things we can do. We can work alone or with others and we can use the medium and style that suits us best.

Remember that a science experiment write-up is really a story – just a rather specialized one. Story-telling is central to so much of what we do. ICT offers all kinds of ways of showing off the finished article (see Chapter 8), but what about using it to make the process of building the story more productive, more inclusive and more fun? ICT-powered story-telling lets everyone have a go at being creative.

ICT-powered story-telling lets everyone have a go at being creative

The Evil Pirate Adventure

The Evil Pirate Adventure began life as an idea discussed between Northamptonshire Literacy Consultants and a Year 2 class in a Northamptonshire primary school. The project was designed to develop and extend children's story-telling capabilities and formed part of the work around link learning modules. Link learning modules were developed by two Northamptonshire literacy consultants with the aim of raising a learner's motivation using dance, drama and, of course, ICT.

Pupils began by spending time on the literacy aspects, drafting and planning the story. These ideas were then translated into a storyboard, which later formed the basis of scenes set up for the digital photographs.

Once the story had been written, pupils set up each scene using Playmobil characters and props set against appropriate backgrounds (these were made using sugar paper and fabric). A number of digital photographs were taken of each scene throughout this process. As with all parts of the project, pupils were allowed a hands-on approach, negotiating how each scene should look and what best communicated their story.

By the end of this creative process, pupils had spent several weeks developing the story and producing a series of photographs that told the story. As part of the progression, they were led through the process of inserting photographs into a Microsoft PowerPoint slide show, adding speech bubbles to scenes. Even at this stage the slides could be re-ordered to achieve the best sequence – a worthy literacy activity in itself.

WEBSITE
CD-ROM

After the visual process had been completed, pupils prepared the narration and dialogue to be added to the slide show. To record the sound a quiet place was found in school – those familiar with a primary school will understand just how much of a challenge that can be! Once the set-up had been arranged in a small room, pupils rehearsed and recorded their narration using PowerPoint and a basic microphone. The final addition of the theme tune completed the package, creating a sense of fun for the viewer. There are many royalty-free soundtracks available on the internet – try Google to search for suitable ones (www.google.co.uk) using the search string 'free sound effects'. The full-length film can be found on the accompanying CD-ROM.

- Digital camera.
- Microphone.
- Playmobil characters.
- Suitable props.
- PowerPoint.

- Photograph toy characters and scenery.
- Use PowerPoint to create an electronic storyboard.
- Add speech bubbles and text boxes.
- Join scenes using subtle slide transitions.
- Record the narration.
- Add a theme tune.

The Evil Pirate Adventure evolved rather than being produced as part of a grand design and was led by an 'I wonder what happens if...' process. One of the key aims of this approach was to eliminate two major barriers to creative work:

➡ Getting everyone engaged to produce the best possible joint effort. Individual paper-based work is about as far from ideal as you can get from this.

➡ Getting started needs to be as easy as possible – high challenge, low stress. It's much easier to start a story gathered around some toys with a camera, as children generally do what you ask them to do, whereas words on paper can be less inspiring.

Holistic learners (big picture people) benefit from the greater freedom offered from this type of approach to map out the whole story quickly and leap from place to place. Analytical learners are able to really get to grips with the stage-by-stage process of realizing the story through words and pictures.

Similarly, looking at the project with a VAK hat on, we have all three preferred styles much more overtly deployed than in a traditional literacy/story-writing approach. The Evil Pirate Adventure has a rich visual stimulus with toys and photographs, the hornpipe and commentary give constant auditory cues and a series of highly tactile tasks are used to manipulate the toys and camera.

This activity also allows some pupils to go off and work on parts of the task that best employ their range of intelligences. This is a common feature of many of the approaches you will find in this chapter; if the task becomes about a leader taking all the photos while the rest watch, the opportunity is gone. In our experience, this scenario is unlikely – one learner with ownership of the pen can dominate a written group-work task, whereas one pupil would have great difficulty managing a computer, a camera and some toys all at once.

Top tips

Story-telling

➡ Mood: use ICT to set the mood for a story. Use audio and sound effects – most movie editing programs have some great ones, and many websites have sound effects you can download for free (run an internet search on 'free .wav').

➡ Characters: a good story has to have characters you can relate to. ICT lets pupils add their voices to characters or illustrations.

➡ Hook: great stories have a 'hook' that you will remember long after you have forgotten all the detail (in The Evil Pirate Adventure it's the theme music). Media lets learners add these memorable details.

➡ Start: those first few seconds bring people in or leave them cold. ICT allows the drafting and redrafting process to really work in on those 'pinch points' – even just projecting it onto the wall and drafting with the whole class can improve the process.

➡ Structure: software like PowerPoint can take storyboarding and make it an essential part of telling the story; for example, create slides with photos, change the order, insert new slides. It can also be used as a browser for the entire story package, enabling the creator to pull lots of story-telling tools together.

➡ Finish: a good story has an ending. ICT allows learners to experiment with alternative endings and to try things out without having lots of extra work to do.

➡ Above all, have fun!

Further activities

▌ Storyboards with digital cameras

The development of digital photography means we can have our finger on the shutter in next to no time, and pictures can be viewed, stored, printed and published at speed and with very little cost.

We know that many people are visual learners (they think and process through visual stimulus), so it's easy to use the camera to aid this process. Learners can make immediate decisions about what they need to record and within a few minutes have the evidence on the screen. It's important to remember that the idea isn't just about taking pictures. It's the application of these pictures in everyday learning that makes digital photography so useful.

Taking pictures and printing them can be a quick process, enabling a hands-on sorting/sequencing activity to take place back in the classroom only minutes after a trip out. To support a geography unit of work, pictures can be taken of local housing materials, landscapes, transport or even the weather out of the window. Other ideas include photos of:

➡ the route to a local shop;

➡ 'who works at our school';

➡ a 'tour' of the school, which can be made into a PowerPoint slide show.

Stories can be told of sports events, plays, school trips and classroom activities. Record growth of a bean seed, a caterpillar, mould on a slice of bread or seasonal changes out of the classroom window. Pictures can be used to tell the story of the walk to school or to record the 'how to...' of a process.

It's important to allow pupils the freedom to use the camera creatively. They will come up with some outstanding pictures to illustrate their learning. There may be plenty of photos that you would not wish to use too, but that's part of the process!

Coming at things a little differently, you could take photographs of an artist at work. These pictures could be used later to tell the story of how the artist worked and the processes used, and to provide a record of each stage that can be used to model working practices to eager learners.

Battery life is still something of an issue, so always have some rechargeable batteries on standby (ideally several sets). Printing full-quality photographs at A4 size may be a little expensive, so you could involve pupils in the quality assessment process of viewing and editing the photographs on-screen before printing. Printing thumbnails may be another solution, as would printing in draft mode. Digital cameras connect to Windows XP without needing additional software, but earlier systems need appropriate software to be installed.

▌PowerPoint as an electronic book

PowerPoint is often considered to be just a presentation tool and it's often dismissed as such when looking for creative ways to record and build stories. However, this software has enormous potential for use as a means to build stories because it has the ability to utilize and manipulate text, pictures, animations, video and colour.

CD-ROM

A little-known sideline that PowerPoint has tucked away in its box of tricks is the ability to build pages that are in effect browser windows complete with navigation buttons, so it's possible to create a powerful interactive multimedia book. An example of a PowerPoint story browser can be found in the accompanying CD-ROM.

Plunder the secrets of PowerPoint

Let's look at the Evil Pirate Adventure, this time told using any combination of video, audio, text and slide show. Imagine our audience is a group of Year 5 pupils who have been set the task of studying the story so far, providing an overview and then deciding which ending they feel is appropriate. The difference is that the task is packaged in such a way that within one resource learners are able to choose a medium suited to their learning style or to use a combination of media to help reinforce understanding.

This can be achieved using each PowerPoint slide as an overview of the next part of the story and a gateway to either more in-depth text, video footage, audio (ideal for visually impaired learners), slide shows (photographs and cartoon storyboards) or links to a glossary. This is all achieved by adding a hyperlink (see page 25) to the title of the item or to one of the ready-made buttons available with PowerPoint.

Therefore, PowerPoint can be used to tie together all the activities mentioned in this chapter in one easy-to-manage file without needing to send learners off to find different resources in different locations. In addition, the original PowerPoint file can be saved as 'read only', ensuring it remains intact. You can choose which linked files are available for learners to edit.

Kar2ouche to model situations and role play

WEBSITE

Kar2ouche is an excellent piece of software produced by Immersive Education (www.immersiveeducation.com). It uses a virtual stage and actors that learners can position exactly where they want, adding speech bubbles (or their own speech) and building storyboards. It's not a world away from the way we use PowerPoint but it offers a few extra features and a simple interface. It also includes educational support packs for various topics – one of our favourites is *Macbeth*.

One of the exciting possibilities that Kar2ouche offers is that it allows a series of scenes to be stitched together. These background scenes can then be developed through the addition of multiple characters, props and sound effects. Once assembled, they can be played through slowly or speeded up to create an animated effect. Using the photographs provided by the program, such as castles, dungeons and woodland settings, scenes can be tailored to match the storyline. The facility to add your own digital photographs means that the story has an immediate relevance to your surroundings, for example using your learning environment for a story about bullying or building a sequence of scenes that take the viewer on a tour of a locality.

Pupils can manipulate on-screen characters to create role-play vignettes, adding thought and speech bubbles to allow the characters to communicate. Kar2ouche also offers the facility for sound effects and speech to be recorded and added to the scenes. Further text boxes can be used to set the scene, add titles and move the story along.

Moving On: Primary to Secondary School is a Kar2ouche pack aimed at the transition between levels in education, although there is no reason why pupils cannot have two aliens or two Roman legionaries from completely different resource packs rehearse a piece on bullying.

This movie was made using Kar2ouche and the Macbeth *education support pack*

Use Kar2ouche to:

➡ retell a well-known story;

➡ explore a role-play situation;

➡ create a school tour using the characters to inform the viewer at key points;

➡ create scenarios for discussion and exploration through drama and PSHE;

➡ bring to life a historical character.

▌ Tell a story to camera

This technique is particularly effective with pupils with additional needs as they can recount the story one phrase at a time without having to learn the whole text. Additionally, learners can edit their mistakes to give a polished performance without feeling threatened.

CD-ROM

For this activity, pupils were recorded retelling a story in various locations and styles around the school. These clips were then edited and joined together. The completed visual story, which is available on the accompanying CD-ROM, shows pupils engaged in their story-telling.

The following steps could be followed for a similar activity:

1   The topic is chosen, in this case the traditional Polynesian story of Maui.

2   Learners write the script based on the story, myth or legend. Speech should be kept simple and direct, with only one or two sentences per scene. Story ideas can be:

➡ saved as a storyboard using PowerPoint or Kar2ouche;

➡ recorded as digital photographs of sketches or mimes;

➡ recorded using a personal digital assistant (PDA), MP3 player, videophone, dictaphone, Tablet PC, computer or cassette recorder. Recorded files can be shared for collaboration by beaming via Bluetooth or infrared file transfer.

3   Select:

➡ varying and interesting locations;

➡ inside/outside buildings, near interesting objects, statues;

➡ locations relevant to the story;

➡ actors for each location and scene;

➡ actors to adopt varying stances (to give variety), for example standing, sitting, leaning, standing on, kneeling, reclining or whatever is appropriate;

➡ which props and costumes to use. Note that props may detract from the story-telling – the strength of this technique is that it focuses on the story-teller. However, the use of an appropriate prop or costume may add to the finished product.

4   Rehearse lines for a short period of time – over-rehearsal can lose spontaneity and pace. If actors are nervous or forget their lines, prompt them by calling out the line and then film/record them as they repeat it back – the extra takes can be edited out. In this case, leave about five seconds between the prompt and the recounting to allow easier editing. It's also worth allowing some licence with the script as some pupils may change the lines slightly rather than saying them verbatim.

5   Film/record in each location. Use meaningful titles for audio and visual clips to remind you of the location and part of the story. For example, '001/220.mpg' will not mean much a week after filming, whereas 'John bumps into tree.mpg' describes the clip in context.

6   Review the footage, re-recording any sections if necessary. Make sure all sections meet the requirements.

7   Edit the footage. Remember that sometimes you may wish to re-insert clips that appeared surplus to requirements earlier in the edit, so permanent deletion should be reserved for really bad bits and the final edit.

8   At the end, a soundtrack can be composed or added to create additional atmosphere, and original artwork could be inserted at points throughout the story or for the title and credits.

9   When you are satisfied with the film, burn it to CD/DVD.

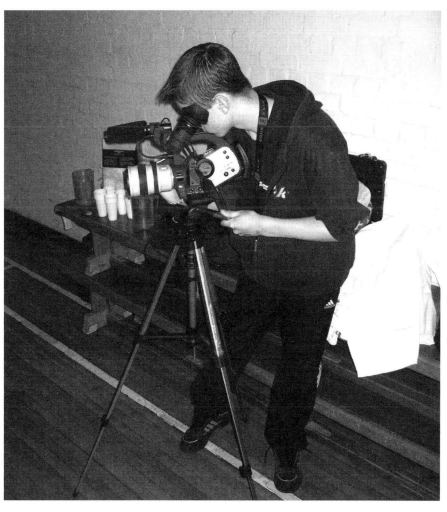

Lights! Camera! Action!

Top tips

Story-telling tools

➡ Projector: a large screen that allows groups of people to discuss the creative process as it happens. Don't fall into the trap of thinking you can make the story on the small screen and show it on the big one – go large!

➡ Headphones: give each learner space to listen to music as they work, and to review audio work time without driving everyone else nuts.

➡ Speakers: we often see a £1,000 laptop plugged into £2.50 speakers – do yourself a favour and get something loud enough and clear enough that people can hear what's being discussed. Tense, mood-inducing music sounds silly on tiny speakers.

➡ Tripod: spare everyone wobbly camera work – a tripod is cheap and useful. You can position your camera and leave it there while you do something else; you get shake-free shots; and you can look like a real media maker for a change!

➡ Microphone: even the cheapest external microphone near the subject is better than the one built into your camcorder or laptop.

➡ PowerPoint: free one of the world's best software programs from the 'dull presentation' ghetto – you can group ideas into slides, link slides together in different orders and create movies from them.

➡ Digital camera: use photos to build your story.

▌Make movies

Making stories and movies are really the same thing – the purpose is the same but the medium differs. Movie making is a rewarding activity although it usually involves more complicated set-ups with wires and batteries. Movie making isn't a one-afternoon activity; if time is tight, try one of the other activities in this chapter instead.

Genre

Before getting the video cameras out, have a think about the kind of movie you want to create with your learners (or let them choose). Not all stories need the full Hollywood treatment:

➡ acting with speech, action, costume and props;

➡ miming with supporting text and/or voiceover;

➡ dancing with supporting text, mood music and voiceover;

➡ puppetry or shadow puppets with text, voiceover and music;

➡ animation developed from drawings or sketches on paper or Tablet PC;

➡ reproducing typical everyday programmes such as television news or sporting match commentaries.

Stimulus

At the start of a movie, introduce your stimuli early. The act of filming itself is rewarding and motivating, so you have to ensure that the story has a greater momentum and status in your learners' minds than playing with the cameras! To introduce the theme, try the following ideas:

➡ digital photos;

➡ pieces of music or songs;

➡ photographs or portraits;

➡ unusual objects;

➡ drawings or sketches;

➡ cartoons;

➡ recorded sounds;

➡ unusual words (for example, *Call my Bluff*);

➡ smells (for example, sea air, warm bread, perfume);

➡ phrases (for example, 'This morning as I was walking in the park, I saw…');

➡ a game of consequences. One person writes the opening paragraph, another writes the next paragraph, another writes the next paragraph. Each contributor can either see the previous contribution or write 'blind'. Sharing via an email loop or beaming works well with this;

➡ setting the story in a new, distant or thought-provoking location.

Story ideas

Highly parallel creative work needs structure so that your holistic learners don't drive your analytical learners nuts!

➡ Most stories have a beginning, a middle and an end, although an interesting variation would be to start with the end and then to trace the story back to its beginning.

➡ Consider a cliff-hanger – a story that leads the viewer to anticipate the next instalment. This allows groups of learners to concentrate on a common part of the story and still have their own endings.

➡ Describe different people's viewpoints or statements as observers of the same incident.

WEBSITE

➡ Mislead the viewer by giving the wrong impression throughout before revealing the truth at the end. For example, use Google (www.google.co.uk) to find mugshots of pleasant-looking people who are actually criminals and people who have physical imperfections who are renowned for their good works. The story could be about assumptions or misconceptions.

➡ Revisit a scene or event a number of times during the film, but each time take the story from a slightly different direction.

➡ Base the story on an object, such as a yellow Rolls-Royce, Herbie or Black Beauty, and show how different people interact with it.

Story ideas can be:

➡ saved as a storyboard using PowerPoint or Kar2ouche;

➡ recorded as digital photographs of sketches or mimes;

➡ recorded using a PDA, MP3 player, videophone, dictaphone, Tablet PC, computer or cassette recorder. Recorded files can be shared for collaboration by beaming via Bluetooth or infrared technology;

➡ drawn as a mind map – create a simple visual map of the concept that every participant can follow.

Planning

Depending on the objectives for making the movie, you may want to carry out some detailed planning at this stage. A template is available on the accompanying CD-ROM to help you to save time with your planning.

CD-ROM

Rehearsals

If you are going to film a movie, you need to rehearse. Rehearsals are actually a key part of the creative draft/redraft process because the ideas that have been agreed on-screen can actually come across differently during filming. Rehearsals give your camera operators a great chance to try out the camera and get confident with the controls without the pressure of getting it right. If you film parts of the rehearsal, you can:

➡ finalize details and review work: does it fulfil your requirements and realize your original creative concepts? Choose a few scenes from rehearsals and project them for the whole class to discuss. This engages more parallel processing, as the whole audience can help the pupils who have made the trial movie, and the whole group can rethink their actions in the light of this. Don't underestimate the importance of this process; small groups of learners collaborating on something have a natural tendency to look inwards and to share a common view of a project, so from time to time it's good to let them see alternatives without making it obvious that this is your agenda.

➡ make final amendments: this is often seen as a 'control freak' behaviour – making the pupils stop before they have started filming. What might work more naturally is to ask each group to respond to the trial movies they have seen in their groups. How do they apply what they have thought about the movies they have evaluated to their own movie?

Filming the movie

Encourage pupils to record alternative scenes before the final decision is made in the edit. A simple clapperboard system, where someone notes down each take, helps learners to stay involved in the editing as everyone has an outline of what has been recorded.

Recording the soundtrack

Music can set the mood for the movie, so by changing the music or recording an alternative soundtrack a sad movie can be made funny or threatening. This lends itself to more parallelism – if you have a few highly creative pupils who are not fully locked into the group activity, a useful outlet might be for them to have two or three additional jobs such as recording a sound effect or choosing the music to be used.

Editing

Editing varies a lot from one type of computer to another, but essentially it boils down to having the right cable to go from the camera to the computer (usually a mini-firewire to full size, but do check before using the camera with your pupils). Plug in the cable and import the movie clips onto your computer. The sequence we recommend is:

➡ Watch each clip, comparing it to your log of shots. Assess whether to keep it or not (this is really important as often what one person thinks is a poor take is actually the best of the lot but the poorest performance by that person). A strategy that might work is to ask pupils to watch the clips in silence, giving them a 'throw away', 'keep bits' or 'use' rating.

- Pull all the clips to be kept into the timeline (usually a window at the bottom of the screen) in the right order.

- Trim off any unwanted bits from the movie. Some learners might become less engaged at this stage if there are more than two using the editing software, so it's a good idea to have a parallel task ready, such as preparing voiceovers and rehearsing them.

- Add transitions and special effects. These can be fun but they can also spoil the film if over-used – it's best to allocate a limited number to each group.

- Titles and credits can be an interesting literacy activity to do later on, or a parallel task.

Fine-tuning

Allow plenty of time for reviewing and evaluating at this stage. If pupils have spent more than ten hours on a piece of work and not evaluated it as they went along, they will not know how to do it at the end by telepathy.

Does the movie realize the aims? If not, make any changes necessary. There is a risk of the show being hijacked by the 'completer-finishers' here. Think carefully – are we really here to make a movie or to learn?

Ask the groups to watch each other's finished work and evaluate it, writing notes on each movie. Use a projector to show the movies to the whole class and ask the movie-makers to note the audience reaction – where did they laugh? Were they supposed to?

Finalizing the movie

When everyone is completely satisfied, burn the final movie to CD/DVD.

▌Soundtracks

Audio or sound can be recorded either when filming the video footage or at a later stage. Different types of audio can be used with digital video:

- Synchronous audio: this is soundtrack that is captured during filming. It's automatically synchronized with the video footage, so if you edit or shorten the video clip the audio will also be shortened. However, there is a trick to overcoming this: lock the video in place, then move or edit the audio separately.

- Narration: this is a separate audio track, which is recorded independently from the main video clip. It's a spoken commentary (voiceover). You need a microphone attached to your computer or camera and, if recording outdoors, some sort of wind shield to reduce background noise. Be aware that when recording outdoors the sounds of traffic can carry a long way and become intrusive to the recording.

- Background audio or music: this can be powerful and set the mood or atmosphere for the film. The same piece of video clip can be transformed from tragedy to comedy by adding a different soundtrack. This is achieved by composing your own soundtrack or by adding one from a source such as a CD (note that you must seek permission from the copyright holder for this use).

WEBSITE

➡ Sound effects: there are many sound effects available that can be added to your video clip, such as screeching cars, creaking doors, sirens and birdsong. Most video-editing programs have sound effects included on the installation disk. The internet also has thousands of free sound effect downloads. Try Google to search for suitable ones (www.google.co.uk) using the search string 'free sound effects'.

Audio settings

For background audio, it's important to select the correct settings before you 'capture' the sound. When using microphones in particular, make sure you select the correct setting that denotes internal or external microphone.

Adjusting sound levels

All soundtrack levels can be made louder or quieter by:

➡ accessing the audio controls on the computer;

➡ using the editing software to alter the audio track in the timeline window.

Fading in or out

There are two options: you can make the volume adjustment sudden and extreme, or you can gradually fade the volume change in (louder) or out (quieter).

Muting the sound

Sometimes you may wish to mute the background music and increase the volume of the speech or narration. Even in basic film editing software the narration and soundtrack can be kept separate from each other and the film, so you have complete control over all the individual elements.

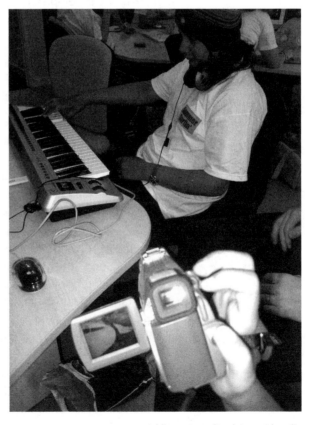

Adding a soundtrack to a video clip

Trimming audio clips

The length of each soundtrack can be trimmed in the same way that you would select and edit the video film.

Composing music for film

➡ Is it a comedy, a drama or a factual piece of work?

➡ Does it have any cultural links? If so, consider using ethnic or world music.

➡ Could you accentuate the key points or heighten the drama by adding dramatic or subtle music at certain points?

➡ Experiment with changing the volume (dynamics).

➡ Experiment with different instruments or vocal sounds.

➡ Consider varying the tempo (speed).

➡ Different sounds can be layered on top of each other to create music.

➡ Try performing the music while watching the video clip, improvising and adjusting the music to fit the film.

▌Hyperlinks

WEBSITE

WEBSITE

A hyperlink is a simple way of telling your computer to go and retrieve a document or page of information. Web pages are full of them and every button or section of text asking you to 'click here' has a hyperlink behind it. For example, visit the Learning Discovery Centre website at www.learningdiscovery.co.uk and click on the text called Contact/Finding Us. This takes you to the page containing the address and contact details of the Learning Discovery Centre. The words Contact/Finding Us are used as a hyperlink object to a new document called www.learningdiscovery.co.uk/about.html. This principle can be used almost anywhere as long as you know the exact name of the file you wish to link to.

In terms of story-telling, hyperlinking opens up a number of useful opportunities. For example:

➡ story splitting: providing alternatives for the next chapter of the story;

➡ linking to related files: taking the reader to other media, such as movies or music files;

➡ providing background information such as 'Gollandos was a Trojan. You can find out more about the Trojans here.'

➡ linking to help areas such as forums, chat rooms and frequently asked questions (FAQs).

Microsoft Word, Excel, PowerPoint and many other applications allow hyperlinks to be added quickly and easily. Use the mouse to highlight the text you want to use as your link, select Insert, Hyperlink from the menu bar, then choose the name of the file or website address you want to link to.

▌Use models and toys as actors

Dolls, toys or objects can be used to represent a character or a concept, or to 'act out' a story in almost any project. Here are some examples:

Symbolism

➡ A rock or piece of crystal could represent magic or a magician.

➡ A coin could represent wealth.

➡ A flower or plant could represent an emotion.

➡ A dagger or weapon could represent war or conflict.

➡ A crown could represent power.

Music or voice links

Dolls, figures or toy animals can be given a sense of character:

➡ Give the characters voices with distinctive accents (for example, *Wallace and Gromit* and *Chicken Run*).

➡ Link the figure to a short musical theme (comic, tragic, ethnic, dreamy, futuristic).

➡ The music theme (*leitmotif*) technique can be extended to imply the character is present even when it is not visible to the audience, or to imply a connection with the character. It can be very obvious or very subtle. For example, in *Jaws* the music associated with the shark is often played before the animal is seen, heightening the viewer's sense of fear and danger.

Toys acting out the story

This can be used with dolls (Barbie or Action Man), trains (Thomas the Tank Engine) or puppets (Muppets).

➡ The toys can be set out in basic scenes and one photo is taken per scene. The scenes can be animated together or left as a tableau with a narrative or text added.

➡ The toys can be held and moved around and filmed live. Add a narrative.

➡ The toys could be adjusted slightly and photographed with multiple shots for each scene to provide more sophisticated animation.

Voiceovers, narrative and music

You can make the film more effective by adding character voiceovers, narrative or mood music.

WEBSITE

WEBSITE

WEBSITE

➡ The BBC website (www.bbc.co.uk) has lots of soundtracks available: search for 'audio clips' on the organization's home page, or look at the BBC Motion Gallery site at www.bbcmotiongallery.com.

➡ Add sound effects to accentuate moments of drama in the story. Search for 'free sound effects' on Google (www.google.co.uk).

➡ Record character voiceovers for each part.

➡ Record a commentary or narration. The accent or character of the narrator can help to add value to the theme of the story (for example, think about public information films, *Monty Python*).

➡ Add speech bubbles and type in text for each character. Why not add a hyperlink to the text in the bubble to a speech recording?

Team writing

There are a number of ways that the all-important drafting phase can be made a truly team effort. You want to achieve this for all kinds of reasons:

➡ motivation: to keep everyone involved;

➡ best use of skills: some pupils are really good at grammar, while others have a good 'turn of phrase';

➡ behaviour: what do the learners who are watching the drafting process do in their downtime?

➡ realism: isn't this how real documents are produced?

If you have access to a number of computers, there are several strategies to keep everyone engaged at the writing stage:

➡ Email roundabout: once you have agreed an outline, break it into equal chunks for each pupil and ask them to write it up. Use an HTML editor like Notepad to save yourself from thinking too hard about which font to use. After an agreed time limit, everyone should email their part to the next person in the loop (the last person emails to the first), and keep swapping until everyone is happy. You can use your network if you prefer, but somehow email or instant messaging (for example, AOL Instant Messenger or MSN Messenger) is more organic. Once the basic story is complete, give everyone a job (either the task they are best at, the thing they most need to improve or a random choice) such as 'grammar guru' or 'adjective avenger' and ask them to reword their text in that role.

➡ Beaming: similar to the email roundabout, beaming makes good use of either infrared or Bluetooth file transfer to do the same job. This is really useful if your writers don't have access to email and opens up participation to a host of text devices such as handheld computers.

➡ Parallel writing: an amazing program called SubEthaEdit (we used it to write this book) allows up to eight Mac users to work collaboratively on the same piece of text at the same time – literally live – with each person's contribution highlighted in a different colour. If you have a Mac, get it at www.codingmonkeys.de/subethaedit and if you haven't a Mac, please pretend you never read this paragraph.

➡ Create a trail: it's helpful to keep tabs on which version of text you are working with, so dating or numbering an edit is a good idea. In addition, keeping earlier chunks of text (perhaps in a different colour or font) means you can always revert back to it if the new material looks less appealing the next morning.

WEBSITE

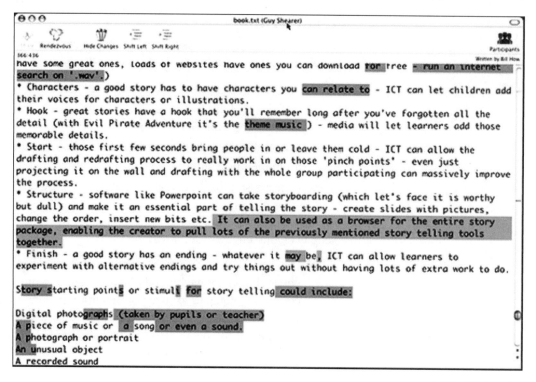

have some great ones, loads of websites have ones you can download for free – run an internet search on '.wav'.)
* Characters – a good story has to have characters you can relate to – ICT can let children add their voices for characters or illustrations.
* Hook – great stories have a hook that you'll remember long after you've forgotten all the detail (with Evil Pirate Adventure it's the theme music) – media will let learners add those memorable details.
* Start – those first few seconds bring people in or leave them cold – ICT can allow the drafting and redrafting process to really work in on those 'pinch points' – even just projecting it on the wall and drafting with the whole group participating can massively improve the process.
* Structure – software like Powerpoint can take storyboarding (which let's face it is worthy but dull) and make it an essential part of telling the story – create slides with pictures, change the order, insert new bits etc. It can also be used as a browser for the entire story package, enabling the creator to pull lots of the previously mentioned story telling tools together.
* Finish – a good story has an ending – whatever it may be, ICT can allow learners to experiment with alternative endings and try things out without having lots of extra work to do.

Story starting points or stimuli for story telling could include:

Digital photographs (taken by pupils or teacher)
A piece of music or a song or even a sound.
A photograph or portrait
An unusual object
A recorded sound

SubEthaEdit in action

Comic-based story-telling ideas

If all this media management seems a little forbidding, there is a really fun way to do story-telling that uses another popular medium: cartoons and comics.

Strictly speaking, there is no reason why comics have to be 'still image', paper-based works. However, there are enough ideas in this chapter to help you make one with movies, so here we will look at still images.

Comic-style writing is easy to do and highly engaging, even for writers who struggle to put pen to paper (or finger to keyboard). It's naturally broken into chunks, has a simple grammar structure (thought bubbles, speech bubbles, 'Kerpow-style' sound effects and captions) and produces results that impress and enthuse.

We find that writing cartoons engages us because we can work in parallel; if we are not sure which words to use, we can move pictures around, resize elements, add bubbles and generally build the story, and often that helps.

WEBSITE

CD–ROM

The quickest route to comic-book writing is to download Comic Life from plasq (www.plasq.com). It's free for a 30-day trial and inexpensive thereafter. Filled with fun sound effects and all the templates you could want, it makes writing comic strips easy. The snag is that it's not for use with Windows. A link to the current version of this software can be found on the accompanying CD-ROM.

A comic strip created using Comic Life

If you use Windows, there are a couple of ways of going for a similar effect with common Microsoft Office-type programs, although they are probably only in the reach of older learners. Make a table in Word, paste into it the photos you want to use and then use the drawing toolbar to add AutoShape callouts for speech and thought bubbles. WordArt can also be used for titles and overlays. Another technique is to use PowerPoint. Make a slide for every box in your cartoon, fill the whole slide with your photo, and use the drawing toolbar to add callouts. When you print the slide show, choose to print six slides per page and voilà – a simple comic book.

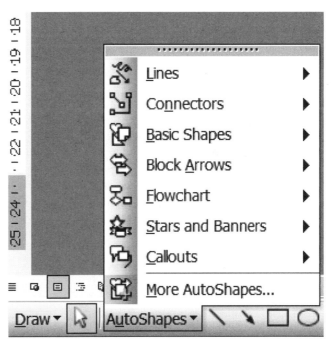

Use the AutoShape function to insert callouts

One approach is to show your learners how to make their own cartoons (with Comic Life it takes seconds – that's why we use it) and let them loose, taking time later to help them relate conventions used in comics to other forms of writing. Another method is to give pupils cartoons with empty speech bubbles in no set order (PowerPoint is especially good for this) and to let them sequence and complete the scenes to build a story.

Top tips

Teaching story-telling techniques

➡ Gather around the big screen: the power of a group throwing together ideas, while a patient soul sits at a computer plugged into a projector and types them up, is hard to underestimate.

➡ Parallel writing: try to give each person a role that plays to their needs or strengths rather than having everyone do everything. Most use of ICT for drafting revolves around the ability to delete things without leaving a mark. Push the limits a little and use the technology to get everyone involved.

➡ Make one and pass it on: get everyone to work in detail on a small section of the story and after an agreed time limit pass it on to the next person. Beaming technology works well with this, as does email.

➡ Actor and author swaps: divide your class into an even number of teams and then pair them up so that each group plays the role of actors to the other group's story. This builds some interaction but is also helpful because it's often easier to act out someone else's words and ideas than your own. It makes the author say what they mean.

➡ Writing as a character: ask everyone in a group to write/plan from the viewpoint of their character (so, with a movie, they film in the first person) and then use the strongest parts of each person's contribution.

➡ 'Here's one I prepared earlier': produce examples with gaps. The example can, of course, provide structure to the story, but it can also give language and images to imitate and adapt. Sometimes we are at our most creative when we see something we don't like and want to change it.

➡ Emoticons allow holistic learners to sketch out the story, emphasizing the mood of each part as it unfolds. For example:

☺ John walked away looking very pleased with himself, then tripped and fell over, much to everyone's amusement.

If this sentence were written with a ☹ at the start, a totally different feeling could be conveyed without getting bogged down in detail.

• Storyboarding can be difficult where there is a boredom barrier, a reluctance to write, or a group dynamic likely to let one person dominate the creative process. Try using mobile phone cameras to generate super-quick storyboards or an MP3 player as a dictaphone in the middle of a group working through a draft dialogue.

Chapter 2

Out and about

There are many learning experiences outside the classroom just waiting to be explored. Away from the organization of the classroom environment, many pupils take on a fresh approach to learning and are prepared to try things they would not ordinarily do when sat in front of a textbook. Stimulation (and distraction) abound outside of the classroom. Likewise, opportunity and occasional frustration due to the limitations of ICT rear their heads away from the school building. However, with the extended life of many batteries and the portability of much of the ICT now available to schools, there has never been a better time to get out there!

The local environment offers many learning opportunities

Many young learners are using a higher level of ICT at home and with friends than within the school environment. These technologies include mobile phones, laptops, PDAs, 3G videophones and Tablet PCs. We will explore the use of Tablet PCs in this chapter and touch on the use of PDAs and mobile phones.

Village schools project

This project was inspired by work with 12 village primary schools across Northamptonshire. These schools are by definition rather isolated and have used mobile ICT resources to enhance and develop the curriculum. In particular, the schools wanted to use their local environment as a rich stimulus for learning.

Each school explored a slightly different aspect of their local community. For example:

- ➡ the school grounds;
- ➡ a local place of worship;
- ➡ buildings of historical interest in the village, such as an old bakery or blacksmith;
- ➡ buildings with features of interest, such as tiles, slates and thatch;
- ➡ a local nature reserve;
- ➡ a reservoir;
- ➡ a museum;
- ➡ members of the community.

Before starting work, the schools were made aware of the ICT that could be used to enhance the project. Once planned, the school then had access to these resources. Working this way around meant that work could be planned knowing which possibilities existed rather than being limited by resources. Nevertheless, this chapter introduces a variety of learning opportunities that can be gained even when ICT access is limited to just one digital camera.

WEBSITE

Schools used their QX3 digital microscopes where appropriate. Using the search string 'QX3 resources' on Google (www.google.co.uk) finds activities and resources to support work with this microscope.

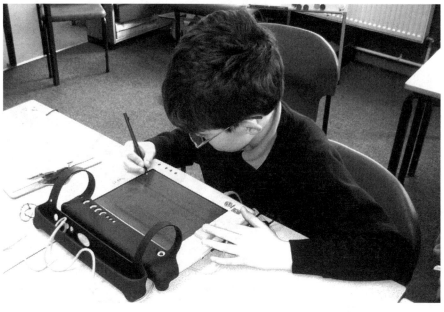

Children found a wide range of uses for pen-based computers

Throughout the activities, pupils were allowed a hands-on approach. They were engaged in the planning and collection of data (for example, images, text and audio clips), which they used in the preparation of a short presentation (mostly using PowerPoint). As part of the progression, pupils were led through the process of inserting photographs into PowerPoint. By the end of this creative process, they had spent several weeks developing the images and producing a series of photographs that communicated aspects of their local community.

- Digital camera.
- Tripod for panoramic shots.
- QX3 digital microscope.
- Mobile phone.
- Tablet PC (with stylus on a string).
- PDA.
- Microphone.
- Video camera.
- Temperature sensor.
- PowerPoint.

- Use a digital camera to collect images of the locality.
- Experiment with camera angles and natural lighting to explore the effect on the image.
- Use PowerPoint or Photo Story 3 to join together photos.
- Add a soundtrack to enhance the scenes.
- Record the narration to add descriptive language to the scenes.

There are a number of benefits to using Tablet PCs that we wanted to explore. For example:

➡ compactness: using tablets in village schools where space is an issue;

➡ portability: rooms may need to have various arrangements according to demand and the subject being taught;

➡ robustness: Tablet PCs are designed to be mobile. Many have cases to protect against those little knocks that are inevitable when taken out and about;

➡ benefits: there are a number of accounts that note the benefits of using Tablet PCs, such as raising enthusiasm and motivation, and keeping pupils focused and on task;

➡ motivation: the use of the stylus when writing directly onto the Tablet PC screen seems to motivate reluctant writers.

Top tips

Out and about

➡ Always carry out a health and safety review before the visit. Take time to familiarize yourself and others who will be leading any creativity with the appropriate procedures.

➡ Check if extra insurance is necessary.

➡ Advance visits and discussions with hosts make for a successful trip.

➡ Establish clear expectations with pupils before you arrive.

➡ Involve pupils in developing activities.

➡ Have plenty of spare batteries for digital cameras and ICT equipment.

➡ Have an emergency contact number for the school.

➡ For fieldwork in a remote area, ensure others know of your location. Remember that in some places there may not be a mobile phone signal.

➡ Use the internet to familiarize pupils with:

  ➡ the venue;

  ➡ the route to be taken – use Streetmap (www.streetmap.co.uk) or Multimap (www.multimap.com). Ask pupils to compare routes via specific points and how long they will take.

WEBSITE ❶

Further activities

▌ Use Windows Journal

Windows Journal transforms your Tablet PC into a digital writing pad. Using the stylus pen, you can write as you usually would and store the notes on the Tablet. The pen thickness and colour can be changed as appropriate. Similarly, highlighter colour and thickness can be altered for the desired effect. The handwritten notes can be converted to typed text later or edited as necessary.

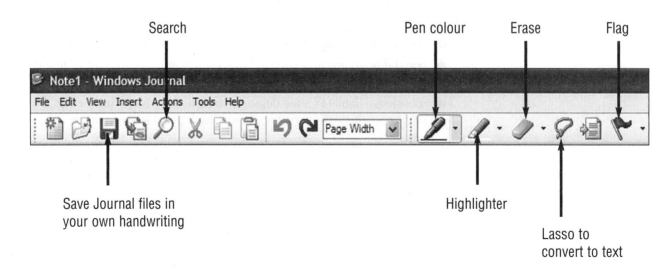

The Windows Journal toolbar

Using the search facility you can easily search through your Windows Journal notes for keywords and recall previous notes. The eraser cleans up a screen or a small section of notes while the lasso feature enables users to circle handwritten text or images and move them around the screen.

Word files, PDFs, graphics, web pages and PowerPoint slides can be opened up within Journal, and, using the pen and highlighter tools, the text can be annotated and emailed on, keeping the originals intact – adding helpful developmental notes for learners in the process. To insert a file into Journal, first open the file. Click on File, Print from the menu bar, choose Journal as the printer, then select Print. The Tablet PC will then ask you to save the original and to bring up a new Journal page with your file inserted ready for annotation. Using this technique, it's possible to create pictures using a graphics package, save them, then import them into Journal to be used as backgrounds for writing.

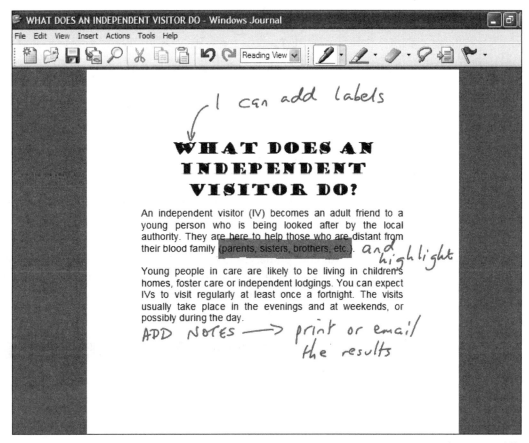

An annotated file

WEBSITE

To read Windows Journal files on computers besides Tablet PCs, download Microsoft Windows Journal Viewer from www.microsoft.com. You will not be able to use another computer to annotate the document. A link to the current version of this software can be found on the accompanying CD-ROM.

CD-ROM

Windows Journal has all the functionality of other text-based software in that it allows you to insert pictures as well as to cut, copy and paste. However, it also allows you to draw freehand directly onto the screen. The resulting images can then be annotated as required.

Similarly, pictures taken from a digital camera can be downloaded onto the Tablet PC, where they can be annotated or highlighted and used directly in handwritten work.

One of the Northamptonshire primary schools we worked with visited the Isle of Wight, taking Tablet PCs along with it. As they were already familiar with Windows Journal, pupils used the Tablet PC as an electronic clipboard – taking notes, drawing diagrams and inserting photographs.

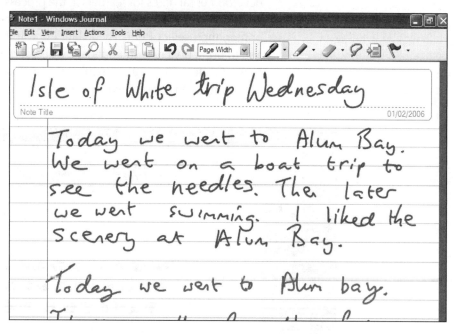

A pupil's notes on the Isle of Wight

Another primary school took Tablet PCs out on a school trip to a local village museum. Again, familiarity with Journal meant pupils used the Tablet PC as an electronic clipboard. Returning to school, they were able to share their notes electronically or via the projector.

Using Journal to annotate photos

Record sound with a Tablet PC

A Tablet PC is an ideal electronic sound recorder. Attaching an external microphone and recording sound clips using a sound editor means pupils can collect images, take notes and record sound clips – either as background noise or interviews. These sound clips can be replayed and further photographs added to create a detailed account of the trip.

WEBSITE
CD-ROM

Audacity is a piece of free software that enables you to record and edit sound files. To download this program, visit www.audacity.sourceforge.net. A link to the current version of this software can be found on the accompanying CD-ROM.

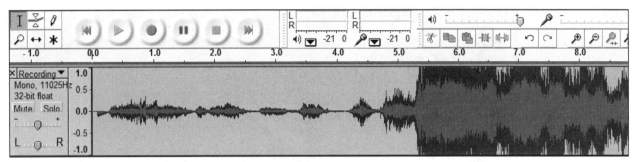

Record and edit sounds with Audacity

Microsoft Sound Recorder can be used for short clips but they are not easy to edit. Open this recorder by going to Programs, Accessories, Entertainment. Choose File, Save As to save your audio file.

Collect data using a Tablet PC

In addition to collecting sound and images, a Tablet PC is a handy size for collecting other data such as temperature. Using software that tracks and records temperature means if you attach a temperature probe to the Tablet PC you can turn it into a mobile thermometer.

➡ Record pond or puddle temperature for a study of evaporation.

➡ Record hot spots/cool spots around the school building. Is the headteacher's office the warmest?

➡ Work out whether trainers make feet hotter than shoes.

➡ Record the temperature of a sweaty hand after PE.

➡ Calculate the temperature beneath a tree and compare it with the reading in the middle of the field.

➡ Work out whether a stream is warmer than a pond.

Some datalogging software also records ambient noise levels in decibels. The attachment of a microphone allows a Tablet PC to become a noise monitor.

➡ Work out whose classroom is the quietest.

➡ Decide whether villages are quieter than towns and explain why.

Using digital video allows Tablet PCs to be used as mobile editing studios. Downloading clips from a camera and recording sound or taking notes means that the whole dynamic of film-making becomes much more fluid and can take place out on location.

Attaching a QX3 microscope to a Tablet PC means that images can be viewed on the screen while on location. Of course, there may be times when pupils wish to use the microscope back in class, but as it can be detached from its base it can be poked into all sorts of crevices!

Collecting data while out and about

Tablet PCs can be used to gather data

ICT outside school

➡ Before visiting a site of interest, download pictures from a website for pupils to annotate while on the trip.

➡ Use photographs and labels to create a montage of key points.

➡ Import a Word file into Windows Journal and use text boxes to organize notes.

➡ If the Tablet PCs have Bluetooth technology, ask groups to share data. If you don't have Bluetooth, a USB memory stick is an advantage when you want to share files between users.

➡ Use Tablet PCs to record sounds around the school. Play the sounds back and ask the pupils to guess where they were recorded.

➡ Record a montage of sounds and join them together to accompany a PowerPoint slide show of photographs taken during the same trip.

➡ Record sounds and match them to photographs.

PDAs

At the Learning Discovery Centre, we have been using PDAs with whole classes. PDAs have much of the versatility of a Tablet PC. In particular, a PDA could be used to record data such as an image or a text-based source. This data could be Bluetoothed between PDAs for quick analysis.

Mobile 3G phones offer users imaging technology. Using the phone's inbuilt camera, stills or short video clips can be stored on the memory card and Bluetoothed to a printer or another computer later. This use of a 3G phone doesn't require airtime as the camera is working independently of a phone call – it does need a charged battery though!

Use Tablet PCs to link back to school

The development of area wireless networks (AWNs) means Tablet PCs are increasingly able to be sited away from the classroom and yet maintain connectivity to the school network or website. Pupils could use instant messaging such as MSN Messenger to feed back data in the form of a spreadsheet or map. They can communicate online to colleagues based at school, who give instructions on where and what information to record.

Alternatively, perhaps some 'treasure' has been hidden in a secret location, with pupils using Tablet PCs to link up and locate it!

The development of videoconferencing means that link-ups could be across the school network, with pupils 'talking' to each other about what they can see and which data they have collected.

Using a Tablet PC back in the classroom

▌ Tablet PCs in geography

This activity can be used to explore maps skills such as 'Where we live' and 'Our locality'. Start by using a digital camera. Pupils tour the locality and photograph various features, such as the post office, church and phone box. These pictures could be inserted into PowerPoint or printed out and sequenced in the order that they are passed from school on a pupil's route home.

Using Windows Journal, a background could be created for the page using a map taken from a copyright-free source. The photographs can be inserted onto the page and sequenced or annotated using the stylus to move them around on the map background.

Pupils could then take the Tablet PCs out on the route to identify the buildings and path taken and check that it's correct. The photographs can be dragged around the Tablet PC screen and arranged into groups according to specific criteria, for example roofing type, age of feature, type of building. Back in the classroom, these photographs could form the basis of a data-handling exercise.

Top tips

Tablet PCs

➡ Keep Tablet PCs charged and ready to go for that unexpected trip outside.

➡ When working outside, increase the screen brightness. Go to Tablet properties and alter the brightness to 'Max'.

➡ Alternatively, change the screen and pen colours to give maximum contrast, for example use a blue screen and a yellow pen.

➡ Connect the stylus by a thread to the Tablet PC. They are not expensive to replace, but a Tablet PC without a stylus is like a desktop PC without a mouse.

➡ Know its limitations: a wireless link across the playground may just work, but a link to the woods half a mile away will not!

Tablet PCs to support history

This activity outlines how a primary school in Northamptonshire used Tablet PCs to support a trip to a local war museum.

➡ Prior to the visit, the teacher visited the museum's website and downloaded a number of photographs of aircraft that would be on display during the visit.

➡ Once at the museum, pupils used their Tablet PCs to find each aircraft and then took notes using Windows Journal.

➡ After returning to school, pupils exported their notes and inserted the photographs to create a timeline showing the development of aircraft.

Top tips

Teaching with Tablet PCs

➡ If you have more than one tablet PC, get a docking station. You can leave this plugged into your projector, mouse and keyboard all the time. This makes it especially easy (and reliable) to hook up any of the Tablet PCs to the projector.

➡ A cheaper alternative to an interactive whiteboard is a Tablet PC connected to a wireless projector. This has the twin benefits of being usable while facing your class and being easy to pass around.

➡ If you cannot get a wireless projector, leave the Tablet PC (or laptop) plugged into the projector and use a wireless keyboard and/or mouse.

➡ To read files created using Windows Journal on other computers, download Windows Journal Viewer from www.microsoft.com. This allows notes written on the Tablet PC to be viewed elsewhere. A link to the current version of this software can be found on the accompanying CD-ROM.

WEBSITE & CD-ROM ❶

Use Multimap to view aerial photos

WEBSITE

Visit the Multimap website at www.multimap.com. Search on your school's postcode and adjust the scale: 1:25 000 or less is ideal. Along the top of the map you will see various options, one of which is Aerial.

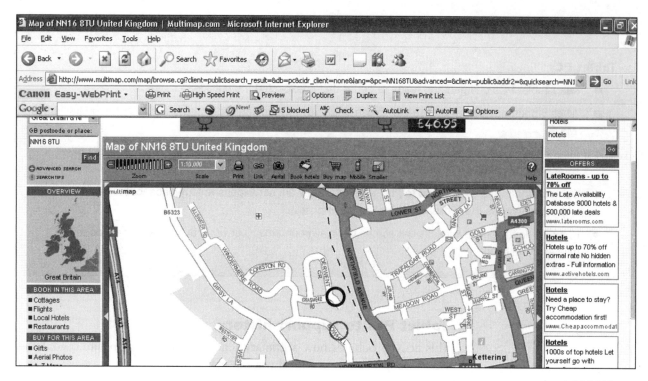

A 1:10 000 map

Clicking on the Aerial option changes the map view to an aerial photograph at the same scale.

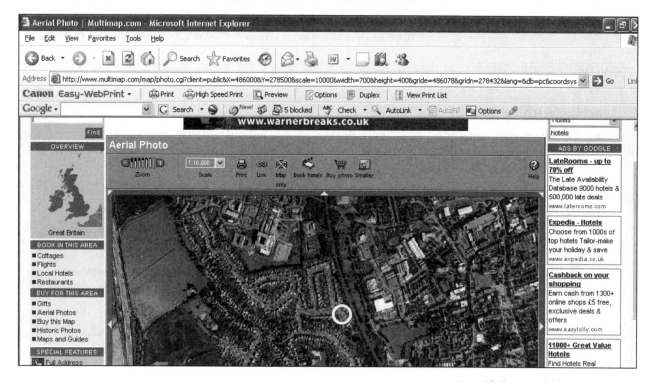

An aerial photograph of the same locality

Hover the cursor over the photograph to superimpose the map. Pupils may be familiar with many 1:25 000 Ordnance Survey map symbols, such as footpaths, roads and paths. If the map is projected onto a whiteboard, it can be annotated and explored by the whole class – the facility to move the cursor over the photograph and see the map 'revealed' is a bit of a show-stopper!

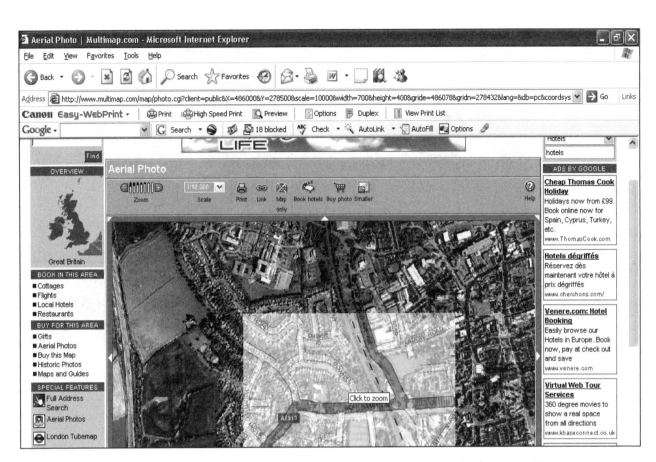

An aerial photograph with a superimposed map

Top tips

Preparing for a visit

➡ Mind map key vocabulary, feelings and tasks.

➡ Ask pupils to list their questions about the day.

➡ Visit the location in advance.

➡ Carry out a run-through of the technology that will be used during the visit.

➡ Hold a videoconference with the host and pupils.

➡ Explore websites containing details of the locality.

➡ Use email to liaise with venue staff and build up expectations.

➡ Pupils could research key facts or establish criteria for reference at the venue.

➡ Ensure all staff and pupils are familiar with appropriate technologies. Check with the venue to identify what skills the pupils are expected to arrive with.

➡ Agree ground rules.

➡ If the event is led by an outside agency such as a space centre, clarify the expectations of the hosting venue regarding learning opportunities, equipment provided by the school, equipment provided by the host venue, skills needed prior to the visit, behaviour, use of first or second names with staff, who has final responsibility for the pupils, lunchtime arrangements if dry/wet.

What equipment will be provided by the school?

Global positioning system (GPS)

A global positioning system (GPS) uses satellites to identify its exact position on Earth. Having this resource available in school makes for a fun lesson and opens up opportunities to teach location and direction in a context not available in the past.

At its simplest level, a location can be identified by its co-ordinates being inserted into the GPS. Once the GPS has the co-ordinates, it shows the direction of this location in relation to the school. This information can be compared with compass points and distance on a map. Some GPSs also allow users to view an on-screen map at different scales.

In-car route planners will be familiar to some pupils. These use GPSs and may also be suitable for use in the classroom.

Geocaching

Geocaching uses the technology of a GPS, the excitement of a treasure hunt and the thrill of hide and seek!

The basic idea is that individuals and organizations such as schools set up caches (secret treasure troves) around their locality and share the locations of these caches on the internet. GPS users take the co-ordinates to find the caches. Once found, a cache may provide the finder with a variety of rewards. All the finder is asked to do is to try to leave something for the cache so that the next person to look inside is not disappointed. Cache sites can be local or require more travelling. For further information, visit the Geocaching Association of Great Britain website at www.gagb.org.uk or the Geocaching website at www.geocaching.com.

WEBSITE
WEBSITE

With obvious application to geography, these caches – arranged around a local field centre, country park or the school grounds – become much more than just the location of a few goodies. They become sites for measuring data such as temperature, light or sound. Using a Tablet PC, this data can be recorded and sent back to school via wireless technology if it's not too far or via mobile phone/text message. Once back at school, the data can be analysed and used as appropriate.

➡ For a scientific or geographical study, record temperature or light. Take digital photographs at a cache site for later analysis and comparison of soil type or vegetation.

➡ For a cross-curricular approach:

➡ Place a sentence or paragraph at each geocache location. Pupils collect the texts to build up the story or poem.

➡ Leave parts of a number puzzle at each location. Pupils collect the parts to assemble later or, to use communication technology effectively, they could text their finds to colleagues at school.

Top tips

Storyboarding

➡ Storyboards can be used to outline a plan of the day, with each scene detailing an activity.

➡ Storyboards can become an itinerary/timetable of expectations.

➡ Pupils could arrange the separate parts of a storyboard into what they think would make the day successful, discussing and comparing the alternatives.

➡ Storyboards could be made using digital photographs gathered during pre-visit work using email, videoconferencing and the internet.

➡ Storyboards can be created throughout the day as pupils collect both digital and real objects.

➡ Ask pupils to create a story of their visit using film.

Follow-up activities

Story-telling
Ask pupils to create storyboards to gather memorabilia they found or created during their visit. These may contain digital media such as photographs, videos or sound files, or they may involve the use of 'real' objects collected on the day. The project could culminate with each learner telling the story behind the memories in their storyboard.

Ask the pupils to create a story of their visit using film.

Broadcasting
With more schools connected to broadband, the results, conclusions and facts gained through a visit could be shared using online radio or videoconferencing. Visit the Radio Waves website at www.radiowaves.co.uk for more information.

WEBSITE

Images of the visit could be mixed with sound files to create atmosphere. These could be shown to an audience with poetry or prose added as appropriate. Pupils could be asked to create a virtual reality tour using PowerPoint.

Photo stitching

Most photo-editing software allows users to 'stitch together' a series of panoramic photographs. This joins photographs on the computer to create one new, extra long picture that can be scrolled through and viewed at 180° or 360°. For an effective series of shots, it's vital to use a tripod. This means that when the camera is moved horizontally it will not move up and down. A video of the 360° view may also be used as well as the stitched image.

Hotspots

Some photo-editing software has the facility to create hyperlinked hotspots. These allow online viewers to click on a particular place on an image and view a close-up, an additional image or another web page giving further details.

Mind mapping®

Creating mind maps helps many pupils to collect their thoughts after a visit. All VAK learners can contribute to the recall of the visit and clarify their thoughts ready for further extension activities.

Videoconferencing

Videoconferencing means that places can be visited and experienced to a degree on-screen without leaving the school environment. Pupils can engage with presenters to explore an environment and ask appropriate questions face to face with scientists, artists and key workers in an area of study. There is, however, no substitute for the actual out and about experience.

A videoconference link between venues

Top tips

Additional software for Tablet PCs

➡ Sticky Notes: a handy piece of software that comes with the Tablet PC. Similar to Post-It Notes and handy for jotting down names, numbers, lists and other details you need to write and keep available on the screen for easy access. You can even use a microphone to record information on the same Sticky Note. This program is easy to see and use – you can copy and paste individual Sticky Notes into other programs, or import and export your entire stack of notes if you like.

➡ ArtRage: a great painting package designed to allow users to work with realistic paints on-screen – without the washing up afterwards! You can download ArtRage from www.ambientdesign.com/artrage.html. A link to the current version of this software can be found on the accompanying CD-ROM.

WEBSITE & CD-ROM ⊙

Out and about with a Tablet PC

- If your camera runs out of battery power, don't forget to take a few shots with your camera phone, and to get anyone else with a camera phone to do the same. The poorer quality may not actually matter.

- If your group has camera phones, encourage them to send photos to you as instant messages that you can then pick up from a web browser – simpler than trying to work out how to get the image out of the phone another way. It's a good idea to have a 'school' mobile to do this from unless you want to give out your personal mobile number.

- If you have only a short period of time on return to the classroom, a photo viewer allows you to share images from the visit quickly without a long technical break to download or power up kit.

Chapter 3

Toys, tasks and teamwork

Using programmable toys to teach in the classroom means learning becomes accessible to all. With toys, we can work alone or with others and we can follow short tasks or build complex sequences.

Teamwork around an organized, structured task using a programmable toy enables all learners to develop their collaborative and problem-solving skills. We also acknowledge the effectiveness of joint creative thinking. In addition, using toys means the learning has a real hands-on feel, allowing kinesthetic learners to be stimulated by movement and direct involvement in a task. The development of ICT offers all kinds of access to programmable toys and machines. This chapter looks at ways of using them to enable learning to be more inclusive – and more fun!

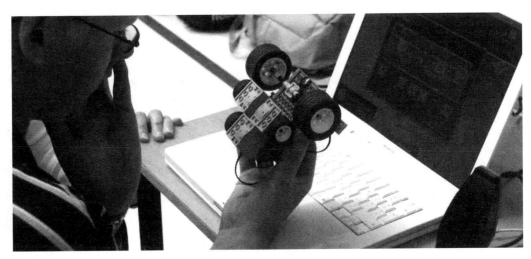

Using Lego gives everyone hands-on experience

It's important to give learners room to explore, create and be innovative in their thinking and approach to tasks. A teacher who gives space and encouragement to pupils to develop non-linear thinking requires a fundamentally different approach. At the Learning Discovery Centre, we wanted to develop a series of tasks that would allow pupils to 'think outside of the box'. Furthermore, we wanted to facilitate the exploration of computer control beyond QCA into an area where pupils use their knowledge and understanding of how to program and work together creatively in order to solve tasks.

Top tips

Toy traps to avoid

➡ Building with Lego can be fun but do think things through first. For example, if you want pupils to steer their robot in a later activity, suggest they make a robot that can be steered during the first activity.

➡ Lego is a pig to tidy up! Sort everything that is needed into a tray and take a photo showing how it should look. Given enough time and help on how it should be left at the end, learners should tidy up for you.

➡ Assembling more complex robots is hard to explain orally. Show slide shows giving step-by-step instructions on what to do, or use cue cards.

Robot Olympics

Robot Olympics came into being as an idea discussed between schools as part of Northampton's Excellence Cluster. This was a cross-phase, interschool event, planned and prepared to create the opportunity for 60 gifted and talented young people – mostly from Year 6 – to explore control technology by completing a series of events.

One of our briefs at the Learning Discovery Centre was to innovate and champion creativity using ICT and to inspire new approaches to learning. To further this aim, we bought Lego Mindstorms Robolab kits. These kits allow for structures to be built in a variety of ways, allowing for creativity. Lego lets constructions be assembled and disassembled relatively easily as pupils explore the task. There is also scope for innovation as pupils test and try new theories.

There is plenty of scope for innovation

Working with Lego wasn't enough though. We wanted to develop a set of tasks that would motivate, stretch and challenge pupils from a variety of age ranges and school backgrounds. Looking for a theme for our challenges – and to add a slight competitive element – we devised the Robot Olympics. Tasks would be set to invoke the spirit of challenge and to bear some resemblance to the games. Models would be constructed to enable competition and team strategy.

Using programmable toys means that:

➡ everyone is engaged so they can produce the best possible joint effort – individual work isn't what we want in this instance;

➡ the activities were accessible for all – getting going quickly means there is high challenge and low stress.

Each Robot Olympic challenge event was planned to fill one school day. The event was held in an appropriately sized room (typically the school hall). Forty-five pupils chose to tackle the robot tasks while a further 15 pupils acted as reporters and tended to have a particular talent for written work. Further reporting skills were developed using digital cameras, videos and by working on a PowerPoint presentation to communicate the highs and lows of a challenge day. We used Lego RCX Bricks but some activities (Olympic torch and freestyle dance) would also work well using Roamers, available from the **WEBSITE** Valiant Technology website at www.valiant-technology.com.

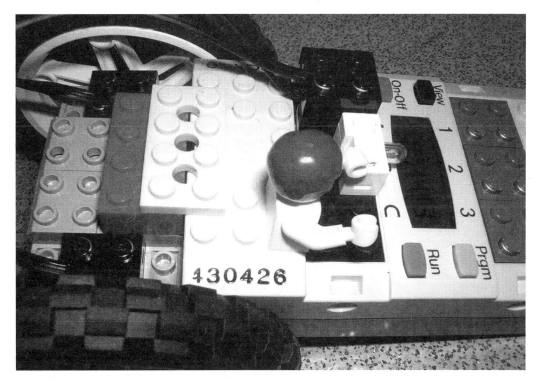

A Lego RCX Brick

Kinesthetic learners obviously benefit from the greater freedom offered from this type of activity. However, challenges also arise for those who are rather more linear thinkers. 'Pen and paper' learners may struggle with the open-ended, problem-solving approach to the following activities – but what an opportunity for learning!

The Robolab software is differentiated into Pilot and Inventor levels, each of which is subdivided into four levels. These enable pupils to get to know the software quickly. More functions and program commands are introduced as they progress up the levels. The software is icon-driven, so there is little reading. Incidentally, it is based on NASA software used to control the Sojourner lander on one of the Mars missions, so it's not limited in its capabilities.

Our long-term aim at the Learning Discovery Centre is to influence teachers' thinking about how ICT can transform learning, and working with groups of youngsters is a powerful way of doing this. By the end of several Robot Olympic days, we had worked with more than 1,000 pupils and 40 teachers. For many people, using control technology is seen as 'hard ICT' – the bit you do because you have to rather than because it has value. We think it's the most incredible tool for building thinking skills, refining scientific thinking, team building – and having fun!

Pupils from each participating school recorded each event in the following ways using digital and video cameras and a laptop:

➡ interviewing key players;

➡ getting the low-down generally;

➡ producing a news sheet;

➡ producing a PowerPoint presentation;

➡ creating a video by the end of the event.

CD-ROM

Examples can be found on the accompanying CD-ROM.

Collaboration

When we work together we achieve more than we can apart, so pupils were organized into groups of three. Each team member was invited to work collaboratively, considering how best the teams could develop and share ideas. Each group had a laptop running Lego Mindstorms Robolab software, available from the Commotion website at www.commotiongroup.com.

WEBSITE

Tasks

The pupils began short familiarization tasks. These ensured each group had the same basic set of skills needed to begin the robot tasks. Learning how to use the software was a key part of the skills base needed. This was done by completing the following basic five-minute tasks:

Task	Activity	Robolab level	Equipment	
1	Turning a light on for two seconds	Pilot 1	• RCX Brick	• One bulb
2	Running a motor for four seconds	Pilot 1	• RCX Brick • One connection wire	• One motor
3	Running two motors and a car to travel 3m	Pilot 2	• RCX Brick • Two connection wires	• Two wheels • Two motors

Using toys encourages learning by experimentation, so once learners understood the basic principles of what the Robolab icons represented, they could modify and control them fairly easily.

Once familiar with programming, pupils designed and constructed small cars/buggies using the RCX Brick as a base, adding motors, wheels and various other pieces.

From the start it was decided that teachers and adult helpers would take a back seat and allow pupils to learn by trial and exploration. This was a key challenge for some adults who could not resist stepping in to 'help' their team!

Main events

The four main events chosen for the Robot Olympics challenge were the sprint race, the Olympic torch, the freestyle dance competition and the javelin/shot put.

Sprint race

Teams programmed their vehicles to travel in a straight line for eight seconds and stop. No sensors were used. Racing lanes were marked out using tape – extra points could be awarded for vehicles that stayed on track.

Using a Lego kit

There were opportunities for plenty of good science here, for example:

➡ Do we go for two, three or four wheels?

➡ Should we use big wheels or small ones on the motor?

➡ How can we keep the wires away from the wheels?

The key aim was to build a fast, sturdy robot that travelled in a straight line. We gave pupils some guidance here:

➡ The vehicle needs to be balanced so that it doesn't swerve or wobble as it runs.

➡ The vehicle should be light but strong and stable.

Creative exploration and discovery are important aspects of the event, so plenty of time must be allowed for pupils to try various styles of buggy. Using stopwatches allows pupils to develop the speed of their vehicles.

Olympic torch

This task was to make sure that the 'Olympic torch' reached Greece in time for the competition! Travelling around the world, the buggy must pass through Asia, Africa and North America so that the torch could be delivered to Athens. The continent shapes were marked out on the floor by masking tape.

A further extension was to design a platform to sit on the buggy so that the torch could be carried securely. The torch was a 15cm length of cardboard carpet tube – awkward and a little unstable.

This task took more thought in programming, relating distance travelled to motor power and time, steering using two motors, experimenting and refining the design.

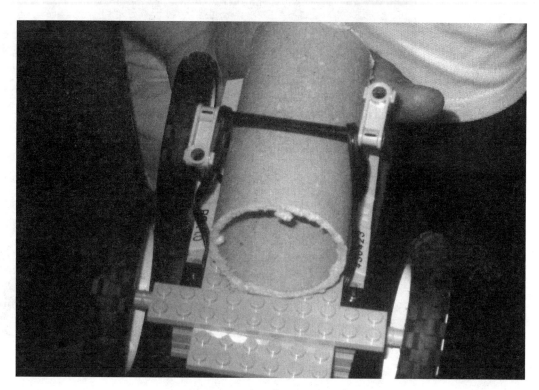

The Olympic torch

The journey was best split into parts. At the end of each part, the robot needed to turn ready for the next section of its journey. As the continent outlines marked on the floor were not straight lines, the most successful pupils built up their program in step-by-step procedures.

Pupils were shown the continents and then worked by trial and error to build up successive steps to enable their torch to visit each place. A further extension was added whereby the buggies had to stop in each continent for five seconds. For this task, Robolab Pilot 4 was used.

Freestyle dance competition

Teams programmed their robots to move around a fixed 'rink' to music. The rink was a circle, 2m in diameter. Robot dancers were judged on criteria such as overall routine, how well their movements co-ordinated with the music, how their design reflected the music and artistic merit. Dancers performed for a minimum of 30 seconds and a maximum of 90.

➡ The buggies had to be strong – dancing places a strain on weak joints! Turning makes them twist in all sorts of directions, causing wheels to fall off and robots to come apart.

➡ The buggies had to be low to the ground so they didn't topple over.

➡ Speed was not an important factor.

➡ A shorter wheelbase made for easier tight turns.

➡ Using front glides or a single swivel wheel meant buggies turned tightly on the spot.

➡ Buggies needed an even distribution of weight so that they didn't do wheelies!

To build up this task, further guidance was given: each movement should last no longer than 0.5 seconds and each move needed to be repeated in the opposite direction while ensuring that the robot remained within the rink.

Javelin/shot put

This was an ongoing challenge with pupils being asked to create solutions to complete the task over the course of the day. The basic idea was that the teams should design a robot arm that could throw a drinking straw (the javelin) or ping-pong ball (the shot put) forward the furthest distance.

Learners were reminded that they wanted height and angle so that the javelin and shot put went furthest. Using a motor and a short time span, the arm needed to spin forward and let go.

- Lego Mindstorms Robolab kit.
- Laptop with Robolab installed.
- Notepaper.
- Laptop for reporting (brought by participating schools).
- Digital and video camera.
- Extension cable (4 x 4 gang plugs).
- Cardboard carpet tube.
- Masking tape.
- Drinking straws.
- Ping-pong balls.
- Music for dance routine.

- Use a digital camera to photograph models before disassembly.
- Use photographs to create a step-by-step construction guide.
- Use PowerPoint to create a record of the event.
- Allow pupils to experiment with designs.
- A 'team' feel can be enhanced by a team name, badge or colours.
- Ensure each team member co-operates and shares tasks.
- Keep the pace moving – make activities brisk and exciting.
- For a greater competitive edge, give points and award gold, silver and bronze medals.

These activities could be developed for the whole class:

➡ Each team could have a budget and items for the buggy could be bought from the teacher. 'Currency' could be earned through a points system.

➡ Ask pupils to create a spreadsheet showing costs, items and events used for construction.

➡ Find out which buggy was the cheapest to make and which was the quickest.

A robot buggy ready for racing

Top tips

Holding an Olympic challenge event

➡ Collect resources before the day begins.

➡ Have plenty of charged batteries available. Rechargeable batteries work out cheaper.

➡ An effective PA system can add to the occasion and prevent a hoarse voice!

➡ Celebrating the event with others in the school raises the profile of a successful activity.

➡ Tables around the edge of the room mean the floor space can be seen by everyone.

➡ Points for loud cheering make for an exciting atmosphere!

➡ Help pupils enter into the occasion by giving teams the opportunity to design their own name, badge or colours.

Further activities

▌Group dynamics

The importance of the development of collaborative skills is taken as read here. What is crucial therefore is the careful planning and preparation of classroom activities that allow for team activities.

While no classroom group is without its leaders and followers, it's important to give pupils the opportunity to try out each of these roles, in this case through the use of programmable toys.

It may be appropriate for pupils to organize themselves into different roles according to their preferred learning style. Examples of roles are as follows:

➡ Project manager – responsible for:

    ➡ setting team goals and co-ordinating information;

    ➡ leading the group through the tasks and making sure everyone understands and performs them;

    ➡ keeping the team on task;

    ➡ asking for the teacher's help.

➡ Communications specialist – responsible for:

    ➡ all aspects of communication;

    ➡ keeping track of all team information in the journal or notebook;

    ➡ writing articles for the news-sheet.

➡ Materials specialist – responsible for:

    ➡ gathering (and returning) all material required for the activity;

    ➡ making sure the correct materials are used in all activities.

➡ Publicity specialist – responsible for:

    ➡ maintaining team web page;

    ➡ uploading graphics and text files to news-sheet;

    ➡ working closely with communications specialist;

    ➡ reporting (text, videos, graphics).

➡ Programmers (everyone) – responsible for:

    ➡ programming the toy;

    ➡ recording progress to enable efficient review.

➡ Constructors (everyone) – responsible for:

    ➡ designing and constructing the buggy;

    ➡ keeping an accurate record of progress.

Top tips

Teamwork

➡ Mix groups up from time to time.

➡ Allow different pupils to lead different tasks.

➡ Ask older pupils to act as a support for younger learners.

➡ Identify learning styles and distribute group tasks accordingly. Discuss with pupils the differences this makes to learning outcomes or to the way the group functions.

➡ Ask pupils to communicate throughout the task in a non-verbal manner, for example by using diagrams or gestures to communicate.

➡ Remind pupils that the success of the team depends on everyone working together.

➡ Allow group members to assign roles to different team members and discuss their choices. Explore their understanding of 'playing to your strengths'.

▌Floor robots

There are a number of educational programmable toys, such as Roamers and Pixies. The obvious benefit in using robots is that, like the children, the robot also goes on a real journey. Floor robots give learners a variety of experiences, such as:

- estimating;
- predicting;
- testing;
- exploring direction;
- exploring distance;
- sequencing;
- observing the effects of commands;
- programming the robot to move along a number line – for Roamers, the units can be changed to match the dimensions of the line;
- using letters of the alphabet to reinforce letter recognition;
- using the robot to teach number bonds;
- programming the robot to follow a command such as 'take the letter to the red house'.

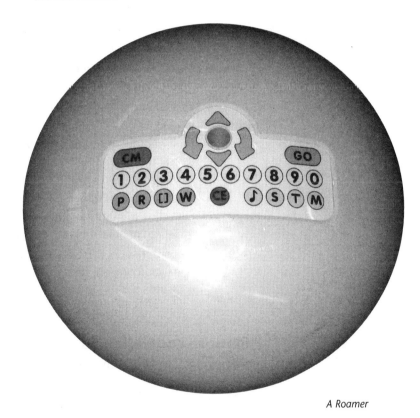

A Roamer

This activity can be adapted according to your pupils. Here are some ideas you could try:

- At the Foundation Stage, floor robots could be dressed up to become a character in a play or story.
- At Key Stage 1:
  - As a simple introduction, program the robot with one step to complete one task, for example to travel 1m.

- ➡ Program the robot to draw a square with 50cm sides.
- ➡ Program the robot to reach the classroom door.
- ➡ Program the robot to take a letter to the blue triangle house.
- ➡ Set up a series of obstacles on the floor and program the robot so that it navigates around them.
- ➡ Program the robot to visit odd numbers/even numbers/multiples.
- ➡ Using different-coloured shapes, program the robot to visit all the shapes of the same colour or shape.
- ➡ For literacy:
  - ➡ Using phonics on the floor, program the robot to spell a word.
  - ➡ Program the robot to travel to similies/opposites/nouns.
  - ➡ Program the robot to sequence a series of instructions.
  - ➡ Use the robot to act out a sequential story such as *We're Going on a Bear Hunt* or *The Very Hungry Caterpillar*. Visit parts of the story in the correct sequence.
- ➡ For other curriculum areas:
  - ➡ Use a robot with a map on the floor (real or imaginary) to create a route around an island and reinforce compass directions, visiting places of interest on the way.
  - ➡ Using a variety of animal or plant pictures, the robot could become a pollinating bee or explore a particular habitat.
  - ➡ Make an activity sheet that has robot directions and ask pupils to predict the shape that will be drawn before trying it out.
  - ➡ Design and make a floor map representing the school, the local area or a park. Program the robot to visit specified places.
  - ➡ Print photographs of famous landmarks from the internet and lay them on the floor. Ask pupils to prepare an itinerary for the robot on a round-the-world trip.
  - ➡ Use the robot to knock a ball into a goal or knock down skittles. For a link to numeracy, the skittles could collect points or have 2- or 3-digit numbers pinned to them.
  - ➡ Explore friction. Measure the time taken to travel 1m on a smooth floor and compare the time taken to travel the same distance across a carpet.

▌ Remote-controlled toys

Before purchasing a remote-controlled toy, it's important to consider the following:

- ➡ price
- ➡ ease of use
- ➡ robustness
- ➡ amount of space needed for the toy to operate.

In some cases, a wire to the handheld remote control unit attaches the toy to the user. This obviously limits you to a fixed distance from the toy, but nevertheless gives younger pupils many opportunities to explore direction and movement with simple left/right and forward/backward controls making direction changes. Sometimes a small wheel on the handset controls direction.

Radio-controlled cars

When using such toys, a course may be prepared for the robot to follow. This course may be as simple as a straight line 'from the red square to the yellow triangle', or it may involve more complex turns and an understanding of the language of direction.

Always give pupils time to explore what the robot can do. In many cases they can quickly begin to develop and refine their approach and test the robot's capabilities and limitations.

The development of simple programmable toys has made the use of robots accessible for very young children. The handset below has only six buttons: forward, backward, left, right, clear memory and go.

A Pixie handset

Using programmable toys doesn't need to be limited to basic movements. For example, the robot could be challenged to navigate through a series of skittles. Some robots can be dressed, with pupils using covers made by the supplier or making their own. Pixie robots can be dressed as cars, buses or animals.

Using programmable toys in the classroom doesn't need to be expensive and, when used creatively, they support many other areas of the curriculum. Watching a group of pupils using a robot quickly provides interesting insights into the way they view the world and are an obvious area of fun and stimulation. Such toys also enable kinesthetic learners to enter fully into the learning process.

Top tips

Using programmable toys

➡ Have plenty of charged batteries available. Rechargeable batteries work out cheaper.

➡ Be creative! Pupils will be eager to solve challenges that are fun.

➡ Use toys to support other areas of the curriculum.

➡ Design an imaginary world for the robot to explore.

➡ Design a town, zoo or classroom for a robot.

➡ Dress up the robot for some added interest.

➡ Design a floor board game using the robot as the counter.

➡ Develop a robot sports day. Explore the possibilities and limitations of different types of robot.

▌Robosapien

The recent development of humanoid robots such as Robosapien means that an ever-wider range of commands is available. These new breeds of robot can walk, dance, bend down, pick up objects and even communicate in grunts!

Robosapien picking up an object

The first version of this battery-powered robot is operated by a remote control and has seven motors that enable it to carry out over 60 actions.

To develop activities, pupils don't need to use the pre-set commands; instead they can explore the possibilities and programs of the robot themselves to make it do exactly what they want it to do. Instructions can be recorded so pupils can follow through their instructions repeatedly and work out exactly which instruction needs to be changed to improve the commands given.

This is a practical activity that requires all learners to collaborate and improve their problem-solving skills:

➡ Ask pupils to work out how many moves it takes the robot to carry out a task. Can the number of moves be reduced?

➡ Build longer sequences of moves to create complex movements. Can other pupils work out which instructions have been set?

➡ Have a race between robots to complete a complex task. Which is the quickest? Which uses the least number of moves?

You can also press your robots into service for more creative projects. A good mini-project is to ask learners to program the robots as actors and to film them moving around in the scenes – this might motivate pupils who are less enthusiastic about programming. Then ask learners to dub voices on top to create the movie.

A more kinesthetic activity with Robosapien is 'robodance' – the device has a limited number of movements so get the group to choreograph a dance for it and invent their own notation system to record the possible moves in order. Ask pupils to rehearse the dance from the symbols without any contact with the people who wrote it, then ask them to perform alongside their robot friend.

Top tips

Using robots and programmable toys

➡ Keep some tasks open-ended to allow for creativity.

➡ Match pupil learning styles to tasks.

➡ Place pupils in unfamiliar territory – those working in an area that isn't their strength can gain a valid learning experience too.

➡ Make learning real. Give problem solving a real-life application – ask 'What's in it for me?'.

➡ Forge the link so that pupils can make connections and apply learning skills to new situations.

➡ Ask pupils to 'think outside the box' and take away the familiar.

➡ Never criticize failure. Failure is success that has not quite happened yet.

▌Electronic voting systems

The use of EVS (electronic voting systems) in schools is fast growing and pupils in all year groups seem to enjoy using them. These systems are based on the use of individual handsets with which they can provide an individual response to questionnaires interactively. A variety of hardware technologies could be used for the handsets, such as networked computers, custom-built wired or wireless handsets (as in personal response systems, or PRS) and, more recently, PDAs and mobile phones.

Most systems come with a bank of questions, but it's also possible to input your own. Many interact with PowerPoint and allow feedback to ascertain pupil understanding.

An electronic voting system

By adapting the questions asked, the EVS allows pupils to give feedback on the lesson. This feedback could take place throughout the lesson and allow you to target the session even more effectively.

Alternatively, questions could be asked before and after a lesson to clarify pupil understanding. For example:

➡ Choose from the following four statements:
  ➡ I feel I have a good understanding of the topic/objective.
  ➡ I feel I have a little understanding of the topic/objective.
  ➡ I feel I have a weak understanding of the topic/objective.
  ➡ I would like to revisit the teaching points again.

Similar questions could be displayed at the close of a session and provide you with useful evidence about how to conclude and how to prepare for the next lesson.

Top tips

Using computers

➡ Even if you have access to only one or two classroom computers, there are still some things you can do to facilitate learning in this area. Encourage pupils to write down their programs before going to the computer or to use cut-out icons to arrange programs away from the computer.

➡ Make sure pupils save their work after it has been programmed. This will make it faster when they go back to make any changes. Use the team roles (see group dynamics on pages 57–58) and assign specific tasks to pupils.

➡ Make arrangements to use other computers in the school.

● Teamwork collaboration can be encouraged by sharing material. PDAs and mobile phones equipped with Bluetooth or infrared allow learners to pass files such as documents, pictures and recordings to each other.

● Use a PDA or voice recorder to voice record instructions for programs or tasks.

● Encourage learners to photograph their progress with a camera or mobile phone. Print off the images to create a storyboard recording and celebrating their achievements.

Chapter 4

Spirit of adventure

This chapter is based on adventure situations in which teams of learners attempt to solve a 'mystery' using problem-solving, exploration and online learning skills, facilitated by the use of ICT. The activities are adaptable for different locations and various situations, and are ideal for customizing according to the local facilities and resources available.

This type of activity is important for learners because problem solving, exploration and research are important in developing independent learners. Learners need to make connections, not only on a neural level but also in their cognitive development. Thinking through problems – linking together clues, ideas and concepts – helps us to come to conclusions and find answers. The methods that support this are exploration, which could be on a physical or mental level, and research skills, which support thinking and provide clues or evidence that lead us to formulate a conclusion.

The task can be adapted according to pupils' individual learning styles; there are opportunities for VAK activities supported by ICT. Learners' multiple intelligence preferences can also be incorporated into the project, with appropriate tasks or roles being assigned accordingly.

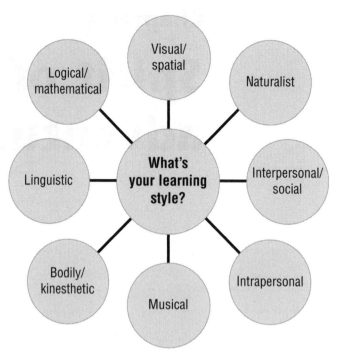

Learning styles

You can build in textual, aural, visual and physical activities to suit the individual needs of your learners. You can work with local buildings, features or local history, or whatever you have available.

Adventure activities can be adapted according to the age group of your pupils. For example:

➡ At Key Stage 1, the activity could be a simple game or puzzle delivered in short sessions to develop thinking skills and problem solving. The resources could be ICT-generated or ICT could be used to record the process, with the data and photos being put together in an electronic storybook or presentation. You could also use this project for a simple field trip or outing to find out about local features or environmental studies. Recording the data on mobile ICT devices ensures a fast result when collating the evidence. The devices can be used to record the findings and download or print it immediately.

➡ At Key Stages 2 and 3, adventure activities are especially suitable as there is lots of fun and physical activity. Investigating a 'crime', carrying out research or performing a re-enactment of an event are all possibilities. Documenting field trips would also be a good task.

➡ At Key Stage 4, learners can use adventure activities as science experiments linked to crime scenes and role play. It could become a whole-year activity using drama, dance, arts, science, and design and technology.

➡ At Key Stage 5, adventure activities could form the basis of a sixth-form team-building activity as part of the induction process. They could also be used for field trips or PSHE days.

How, where, when, why, who, what?

For this activity, pupils were given a focus or starting point. For example:

➡ a castle
➡ a museum
➡ a theatre
➡ a local old property
➡ a landscape feature
➡ an art gallery
➡ a famous painting
➡ a local historical crime
➡ a historical event
➡ an artefact
➡ a photograph from local or national archives.

Ideas for starting points

Pupils had to answer the following questions about the item at the centre of their investigation:

➡ How?

➡ Where?

➡ When?

➡ Why?

➡ Who?

➡ What?

They carried out research to provide evidence to support their conclusions. The research involved:

➡ field trips to relevant locations;

➡ studying maps, county archives, libraries and museums;

➡ interviewing local residents or people with specialized expertise or knowledge;

➡ holding videoconference links with various experts;

➡ studying photos, videos, online records, archives and audio recordings of people being interviewed.

Teachers, parents and drama students dressed in costume and role-played characters related to the theme. This gave learners additional information and helped them to make the necessary links and connections while developing interview skills such as learning to ask the right type of questions.

▌Main activity

➡ Select the local object, building or feature at the centre of the investigation.

➡ Decide on or create the storyline to be researched. It could be that the object is related to a crime, a famous person has links to the object, or something dramatic occurred at the chosen location.

➡ Write and prepare character scripts.

➡ Brief the character actors.

➡ Liaise with the local library, museum and county archives.

➡ Find and edit newsclips to provide background information or to set the scene. Try the British Pathe film archive website at www.britishpathe.com.

WEBSITE

➡ Set up science, chemistry and forensic experiments, such as fingerprints, footprints, paint, trajectories of falling objects.

➡ Use lemon juice to write on paper. Heat the paper in an oven to reveal secret messages, coded letters, anagrams and number puzzles. Pupils have to crack a code to access the safe.

➡ Set up a wireless network/base or computer room.

➡ Provide the control team with a selection of reference material and suggested websites to help them to direct the field team's activities.

➡ Use ICT linked to a wireless network to record and research data. Use phones to provide communication links. GPSs can plot the field team's activities.

Tools

- Video phone.
- Video camera.
- Digital camera.
- Tablet PC.
- PDA.
- GPS.

Key Points

- ICT can be a means as well as an end – just because the use of ICT is a novelty and simply enhances atmosphere doesn't mean it's not valuable.

- ICT can be used to contact people not normally accessible to learners – these people may, of course, be fictional. The use of ICT can help to make something more authentic.

- Quality literacy and numeracy outcomes can come from what is essentially a game, with ICT providing the 'hook' as well as the tool to realize ideas.

- A game or competitive element can be introduced to solve each part of the mystery. This could include clues that lead learners to the next stage; conundrums and puzzles to be solved before they can unlock the clue to the next step; anagrams; maths problems; any puzzle that requires problem-solving and thinking skills. It could also be an activity to perform a dance or a ritual.

This type of task works well with a maximum of six pupils in each group: four out doing field research and two back at the control room with internet access to carry out research and collate data. You could have five teams, each starting from a different location or with a different aspect of the activity. This ensures teams work independently.

▌Possible end results

➡ Lots of data and evidence will be produced, showing each learner's progress and achievements.

➡ A reward, if appropriate, could be offered for solving the mystery or given for the best presentation or research.

➡ Pupils could prepare and give a presentation using PowerPoint. Alternatively, they could perform a 'Poirot-style' summing up – with video flashbacks – about their investigation, describing the evidence found together with data and conclusions. This presentation could be done at a subsequent assembly or a special evening involving parents.

For this activity, the emphasis is on having fun and being physically and mentally active. We know that if learners are enjoying the activity, they will learn more effectively, retaining knowledge and being happy to recall the experience. ICT and communication skills are integral parts and enable learners to access information quickly and effectively

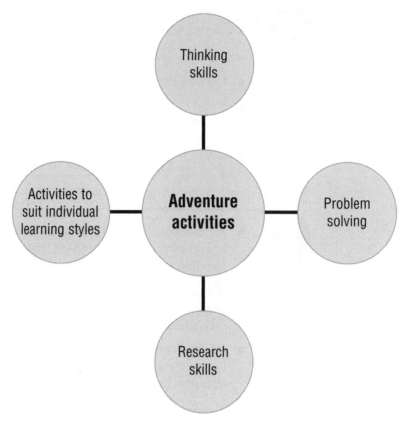

Key components of adventure activities

Teamwork and group dynamics are important. This type of project can be used as a vehicle for team building, developing social skills and assigning individuals either according to their strengths or to help them develop new skills.

➡ Teamwork is an important element and is crucial to a successful outcome for this type of activity.

➡ Joint creative thinking is also a key factor, with brainstorming ideas triggering new lines of thinking.

➡ ICT and mobile devices enable the team to function more efficiently and over a greater distance, while using mobile 3G phones speeds up the flow and collection of data.

Top tips

Teamwork

➡ Mix groups up from time to time.

➡ Allow different pupils to lead different tasks.

➡ Ask older pupils to act as a support for younger learners.

➡ Identify learning styles and distribute group tasks accordingly. Discuss with pupils the differences this makes to learning outcomes or to the way the group functions.

➡ Remind pupils that the success of the team depends on everyone working together, even if they are in different locations.

➡ Allow group members to assign roles to different team members and discuss their choices. Explore their understanding of 'playing to your strengths'.

Possible learning outcomes

➡ Learners are given the opportunity to 'be someone else' in order to empathize with historical or fictional characters – to 'walk in someone else's shoes'. This can be a powerful and profound experience that can help to internalize learning and understanding.

➡ Another possible outcome is that pupils think several steps ahead of their present situation, leading to their considering the consequences of their actions.

➡ Learners also think about what is relevant to the situation and the context in which they are working.

➡ They develop a sense of purpose and direction to their research and learning, finding that each step leads them to the next.

➡ It's also an opportunity to have fun and excitement while learning and developing as a learner. This aids memory recall and provides a stimulus and desire for future learning.

➡ Teamwork is an outcome that helps the development of social and life skills while allowing peer mentoring and support to take place.

➡ Problem solving is inherent to this type of activity, allowing learners to 'think outside the box', finding new and varied solutions to problems.

➡ To enable learners to solve problems, thinking skills are required – connecting concepts and ideas, exploring new possibilities, looking at facts or objects in a different light or from a different perspective.

➡ Learning and developing new research skills allows learners to gain information that allows them to think through the problem, solve it and reach a conclusion.

➡ By utilizing ICT in new and innovative ways, learners increase their skills and the overall effect of all these positive learning experiences develops their confidence, making them more independent and helping to engender a greater love of learning.

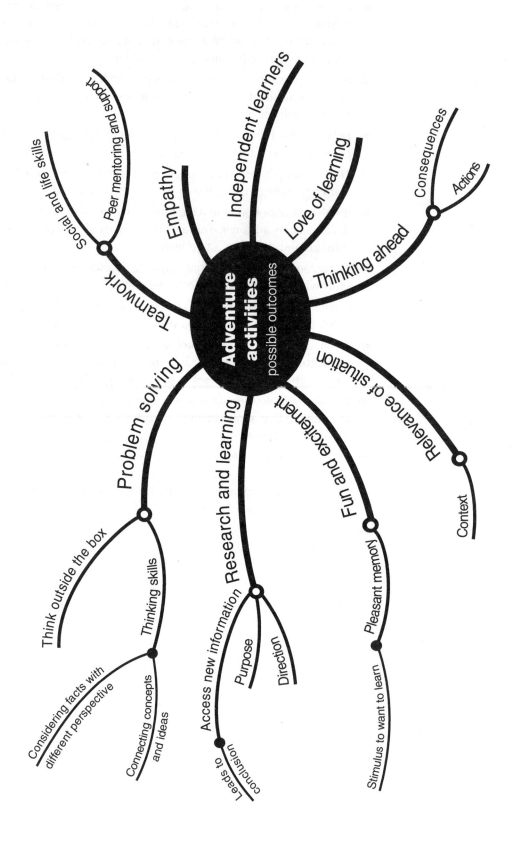

Possible learning outcomes

Using ICT appropriately and effectively

➡ ICT can be used to set the mood for the adventure.

➡ It can facilitate links on a national and international level; videoconferencing allows learners to access the views and knowledge of a professional expert or to view museums or artefacts in other places.

➡ Learners can also access virtual tours of exhibitions. Videoconferencing using 3G videophones provides a link for the field team to report back to the control centre.

➡ ICT can be used to create computer-game environments or to make clues, puzzles or sound tracks to enhance the activities.

➡ Internet research, online census reports and news articles can all be used to good effect.

Further activities

Solve the mystery

1 A crime has been committed! A priceless silver statue presented to the school by a past student has gone missing. It was last seen in the headteacher's office at 2pm on Friday. School finished at 3.30pm. The headteacher's secretary noticed it missing at 4pm.

2 On checking the headteacher's office, it is found that only the silver statue is missing. There are blue footprints on the carpet, and there is a white powder substance on the desk. All the doors and windows are locked. Only the headteacher, the caretaker and the secretary have keys to the office.

3 Collect evidence:

➡ Ask teachers and parents to dress up as character roles.

➡ Collect evidence using PDAs, Tablet PCs, dictaphones, iPods, and digital and video cameras.

➡ Brief pupils on how to ask 'open' questions. Practise their interview technique. Digitally record or note statements (video camera or 3G phone could be used).

4 Interview notes:

➡ Mr Pavarotti, the music teacher, was taking a music rehearsal between 3.30pm and 4.30pm in the school hall opposite the head's office. He heard a crash and noticed that the door of the office was open at about 3.45pm.

➡ At 3.30pm Dr Faraday, the head of science, was knocked down by someone in a teacher's gown running out of the chemistry lab. A jar of sucrose granules was reported as missing.

➡ Miss Rembrandt, the art teacher, reported some art materials were missing.

➡ Mrs Shakespeare, the English teacher, also reported hearing a crash but thought she saw a person in a teaching gown running away from the headteacher's office.

5 Lab tests of chemicals and substances in head's office:

➡ White substance: tested as sugar.

➡ Blue marks: tested as ink.

➡ Footprints: photographed and all shoes of suspects checked.

➡ Fingerprints: taken and cross-referenced with staff and visitors.

➡ Photos: taken of head's office and other relevant areas.

6 Internet research on the silver statue and the benefactor using various search engines.

7 Videoconference link to auction house expert. This could be a parent, teacher or sixth former in another part of the school.

8 Research background information about the statue, such as its history and value, whether it could be sold and what sort of person would buy it.

9 Virtual visit to museum websites to see similar objects.

10 Team members meet to share and discuss evidence and clues. Look at photos, interviews, review the crime scene. Do they have all the evidence? Do they need to interview again any of the key witnesses?

11 Prepare a presentation of all the evidence. Use PowerPoint to create a slide show. Make mini films for flashback video of interviews and replays.

12 Preparing the school hall:

➡ Pictures and displays set up around hall or in the foyer.

➡ Set up a projector to show digital photos and videos.

➡ Parents, students, teachers and actors assembled.

➡ Investigation team presents findings on the stage.

➡ Main suspects are also seated on the stage.

13 Considering the evidence:

➡ Pupils go through the evidence and lead the audience through the investigation.

➡ Each suspect is considered.

14 Summing up. The culprit is named and, using video flashbacks or photos, the crime exposed. Possibly the headteacher has had the statue in her pocket all along and has forgotten she picked it up!

Top tips

Adventure activities

➡ Ensure good communication between teams.

➡ Supervise the teams and guide them rather than direct them in their research and conclusions.

➡ Investigate local facilities and resources to gain maximum benefit from the experience.

➡ Try to match individual learning styles to the type of activities.

➡ Ask pupils to collate findings and present them to an audience.

➡ Include puzzles, games and practical activities.

➡ Have fun!

Spymaster

The resources required for this activity include:

➡ a Tablet PC equipped with Microsoft Office and Audacity;

➡ a photograph of the 'spy' split into sections;

➡ sections of a similar photograph – false clues;

➡ web pages containing the picture components;

➡ a template that allows the component parts to be assembled using PowerPoint.

This is an exciting challenge that uses the journey towards the answer to a puzzle as the learning experience. With modifications to suit age and ability, this activity can be valuable to learners from Year 1 through to sixth form. This example has been developed for Year 7, but it could be adapted easily to other settings.

CD-ROM

The key to the success of this activity lies in setting the scene. Gather in a darkened room. You will need some audio and visuals to establish that the learners are 'in training' for an intelligence agency. We have included some examples on the accompanying CD-ROM to help you design your own.

CD-ROM
CD-ROM

Play a sound track (an example can be found on the CD-ROM) to set the mood. The accompanying CD-ROM also contains an image we used to form a logo/brand – in our case we took our schools service logo and modified it.

CD-ROM

Then play a set of instructions for your code breakers. The CD-ROM contains four examples of audio 'messages from the director'. These were recorded in Audacity and slowed down by 10 per cent to make them sound like they have been distorted to hide the identity of the speaker. The instructions obviously vary depending on the route you want learners to follow, but this example was one of a number we have used.

CD-ROM

After the audio messages have been played, the class should be given clues in an envelope. On the CD-ROM we have included a number of examples to give you some ideas. As learners complete the clues, the answers they reach will be numbers. Each number is the last part of a website address, which takes them to a web page containing the first picture component making up the face of the enemy agent. Again, examples of photo fragments are available on the

CD-ROM

CD-ROM, but you may wish to replace the photo with one showing someone familiar at your school.

Each photo fragment is saved until the whole picture can be assembled at the end of the challenge. These steps are repeated until all clues have been found.

The picture components could be assembled on a previously generated puzzle page and the teams could go on to report the identity of the 'spy' using a special email address.

The spymaster activity provides a framework for many similar scenarios that could work for a range of curriculum areas. Here are some further examples you could develop according to your own situation.

Find and replace

We have intercepted a message from the enemy but it appears to be junk. We know that a coded message – probably numbers – is hidden in there somewhere, but the message is long!

The message consists of numbers that have been coded using a simple substitution code (a = 1, b = 2, etc). When decoded, the word gives a website address containing part of the photo. The ICT skills involve using the find and replace function in a word-processing program.

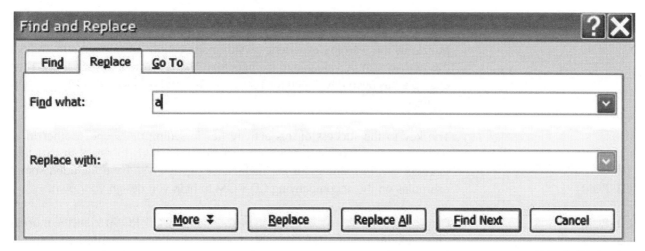

Using find and replace

The captured sound

We have successfully tapped the phone line of an enemy spy and captured the following sound, although he appears to have used some trick or other to scramble it to make it hard to understand.

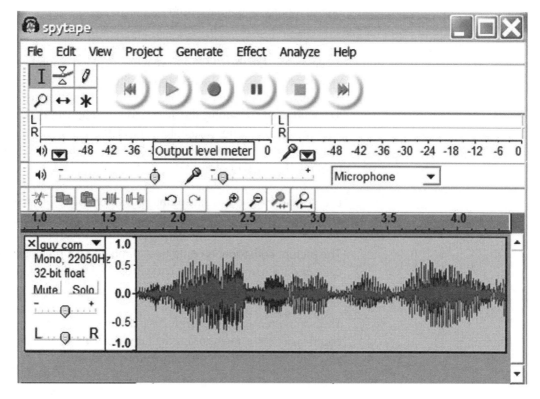

The captured sound

The message is an audio clip giving a website address that has been modified in Audacity. Solving the message relies on trial and error – it will certainly help if a number of code breakers each has a laptop and headphones so they can work in parallel.

It's in the edit

We know the text we found in this email to enemy headquarters has a message hidden in it, but have no idea what it might be. Help!

This is a literacy activity. The key is that within the long and seemingly innocent text are errors – either grammatical or spelling – giving information about the web page containing the next part of the picture. A quick solution is to use the spell checker!

Image editing tools

An enemy agent nearly died trying to stop us getting this picture. It must be important, but we can't see why.

The website address containing the next part of the photo is hidden very small in the picture. While learners could spend ages zooming in at random trying to find the text, you could either:

➡ give them a clue about the location from something enigmatic the spy said during interrogation;

➡ ask them to use image editing tools to make the words stand out (for example, reducing the red and green levels in the photo reveals the hidden word clearly).

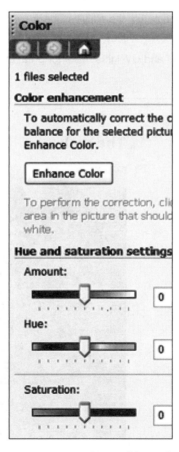

Image editing tools

Hidden clues

We know the spy has been leaving messages somewhere in this room, but we're not sure how he does it. We have this portable ultraviolet lamp you might want to use.

Hidden around the classroom are a series of clues written in invisible ink. Armed with a handheld UV light, the spy catchers collect the clues – which could be number problems, hidden or misspelled words. It is usually better to write the messages on surfaces like glass.

Orienteering by numbers

A spy has been caught with this mobile phone, but we need your help to work out what information we can get from it.

Using mobile phones, the code breakers are provided with an SMS text message containing a map reference giving the location of the first message. Each message contains a number problem, the answer to which is sent back to headquarters for conversion to the next map reference. If the answer is incorrect, a message tells the team to try again. The final location identifies the website address containing the next part of the photo.

Top tips

Things to avoid

➡ Think carefully about where extra excitement and atmosphere help and where they might hinder learning.

➡ Be sure to debrief learners.

➡ Recap on the processes of learning and the main points to ensure pupils' primary memory is one of learning.

➡ A technical fault can ruin the activity. Check everything in advance and have a contingency plan. Explain any technical glitches as part of the scenario.

➡ Smoke machines and UV lights make for great atmospherics, but think through any safety issues in advance.

▌ The wall

The wall

The photograph on page 80 shows the remains of a wall in a local park. Ask pupils to study a similar photograph of a ruin or historical site in your locality and to answer the following questions:

- ➡ How was it built?
- ➡ Where is it?
- ➡ When was it built?
- ➡ Why was it built?
- ➡ Who built it?
- ➡ What is it?

Split the class into two teams: the field team and the control room team.

Ask the field team to take photos of the subject. If they are using a 3G phone, they could send photos to the control room. If they are using digital cameras, store the images for later use. Pupils use Tablet PCs or PDAs to make notes about the location and geography of the site, and to make a detailed sketch of the subject.

Back at the control room, the team could research the location by looking at maps and historical records on the internet. Ask them to research the type of building materials used and how it was constructed.

Meanwhile, the field team could visit the local museum to acquire further information, asking for contact details of local experts or historians. Have there been any archaeological excavations of the site? If so, what did they find? Pupils could take photos of evidence and findings.

In the control room, pupils could arrange a videoconference with a local, national or international expert, or a national museum or specialist centre. Record the videoconference session.

The field team returns to base and the whole team could try building a miniature version of the subject. Were the construction and design good? What did they find out about the materials used? Were they strong enough and suitable for the job? Would it have been easy to build the original version? Why was the ruin or building needed? Video these discussions.

When the learners have carried out their research, ask them to gather all the evidence together. They need to collate their findings and put everything together in a presentation. This could take the form of a:

- ➡ display area – ideally with a board showing photos and videos – surrounded by stone samples and sketches;
- ➡ PowerPoint presentation in assembly for fellow students and parents;
- ➡ Roman day with food specialities, dressing up and a re-enactment to show how the wall was built;
- ➡ radio broadcast using sound clips from interviews, observations from students and commentaries;
- ➡ film documentary with sound/music, voiceover commentary and subtitles;
- ➡ website article;
- ➡ scrapbook or PowerPoint 'talking' book;
- ➡ drama, dance, musical composition, painting, poem, short story or play based around the findings of the activity and using the knowledge researched to give it authenticity.

➡ The wall in this case is actually the remains of a Roman wall dating back to the second century AD. It was part of the original wall that encircled a Roman city that once existed on the site.

➡ It was built in layers using local flint set in cement then a layer of terracotta tiles.

➡ It was not easy to build as it needed a wide base to make it strong.

▌ Research an artefact

What is this object?

Obtain a photograph of an unusual object. For this example we used a silver sugar shaker. Ask pupils to study the photograph and answer the following questions:

➡ What is it?

➡ What is it made from?

➡ Who made it?

➡ Do the engravings have any significance?

➡ When and where would it have been used?

➡ Who would have used it?

Split the class into two teams: the field team and the control room team.

The field team:

➡ visits a local museum, antique dealer, auction house or silversmiths;

➡ researches the maker's mark before contacting the control room team and asks them to research the maker. How was it made?;

➡ considers whether it was beaten into shape or poured into a mould;

➡ discusses how they think the engravings were made.

The control room team:

➡ is based in an ICT room with internet connection and access to a library (real or online);

➡ researches information on silver tableware, looking up date and maker's stamps.

Both teams meet up to compare their information. If possible, link the work to a practical activity for kinesthetic learners. For example, make a similar object out of clay, Plasticine or Play-Doh and use it to engrave patterns onto. What methods or problems would the maker have had to deal with?

▌ Email/webcam investigation

Set up two teams of students: an older team of witnesses and a younger team of investigators. Alternatively, set up two teams with a mix of age ranges.

Tell the learners that a crime has been committed, but the only way the witnesses can be interviewed is by email or webcam.

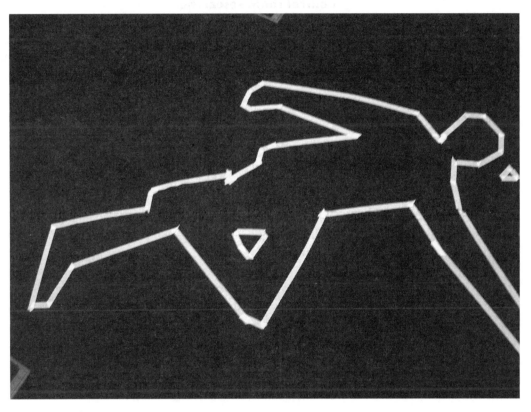

This crime needs to be solved!

➡ The witnesses are briefed and each person assigned a role. They need to empathize with the character and behave accordingly.

➡ The investigators are given an outline of the crime and details about what has happened, together with photos and evidence.

➡ The investigators work together to make a list of questions they wish to ask the witnesses and the research information they will require in order to be better informed.

➡ Each investigator takes on a task: to email or speak on webcam to a witness, or to research information using the internet.

➡ When they have gathered all their evidence, the investigators meet to discuss the evidence and agree on who, why, when and how the crime was committed.

➡ The investigators put together a summary of questions, answers, evidence and research to explain how they came to their conclusion.

➡ All the evidence is collated and made into a presentation.

Group dynamics

Allow pupils to try out different roles according to their learning styles. This activity would work with a few desktop computers with internet access or with a wireless network set up on location.

Control room manager

This role requires a person to oversee the control room and field teams. They have to be aware of the bigger picture. This role may need adult supervision to help guide a younger learner, but the adult should not direct or tell the learner what to do. Someone with good organizational and communication skills would be ideal for this role.

Control room researcher

This role requires a person to communicate with the field team, liaise with the manager and search the online research facilities available for the required data. This role would suit someone who can work independently and use initiative (or work with adult supervision on assignments).

Control room collator

This role would suit someone who can work quietly and methodically, logging all the data, and recording and storing it. They could also prepare materials for the final presentation.

Field team leader

This role requires quick thinking, leadership qualities and good communication skills. It would suit someone who can stay cool under pressure and use their initiative.

Field team photographer

This role would suit someone who enjoys practical activities.

Field team evidence recorder

This role would suit someone who enjoys writing and recording verbal evidence. They need to have good interpersonal skills, and be able to communicate clearly and effectively.

Top tips

Adventure enhancers

➡ Any way of allowing groups to 'spy' on one another deepens the sense of immersion – webcams or audio recordings are especially useful.

➡ Simple things like 'white noise' on televisions can add a slight edge.

➡ Even familiar places can be made to seem different with smells – incense or perfume, or the smell of solder or burned matches, can make a room feel different and perhaps slightly dangerous.

- With many adventure-oriented activities, capturing the learning moment and recording progress is key to developing continuity and further learning. Try using camera phones or MP3 recorders to keep a visual or audio record of progress.

- Wireless PDAs or mobile phones can be used instead of PCs to access material such as the web-based clues in the spymaster activity and lend themselves well to activities where extreme mobility is an advantage.

- Audio clues could be generated as MP3 webcasts or podcasts for download onto a student's own MP3 player or iPod.

Chapter 5

Outside-in creativity

This chapter is about bringing stimuli in from outside the creative classroom. It follows a simple premise: the more we set up opportunities for people's creative sparks to fly, the more ideas will flow, and once the process starts you will not have to work hard to keep it going.

Creativity can be as much about finding things out (especially when we make that deductive 'leap') as it can be about expression, and this is the main aim of this chapter. In the creative classroom we aim to get past the facts and get on to understanding.

Letting the outside in offers the chance for learners to browse from a menu infinitely longer than the one inside – and no matter how meticulous or inspirational you are, what is on offer outside adds a whole dimension of freshness. Here are some suggestions for bringing the outside in:

➡ Invite visitors to talk to, interview and record. They can be there in person (right here, right now – authentic but difficult to set up) or online and on-screen (sterile but controllable). Both types of interview can be recorded and used when needed.

➡ Bring in objects and artefacts as alternatives to people – again, the real thing can be replaced with digital alternatives.

➡ Search the internet and see what you can find online.

Digital video without cameras

All we needed for this project was a broadband connection to the National Education Network and a PC running Windows XP, which includes Windows Movie Maker. If you are using a Mac, iMovie will work too.

WEBSITE

▌ Step 1

We used the British Pathe film archive website at www.britishpathe.com for our research. Because the site is so large, it was worth planning the kinds of words the class used as search terms. The theme of our film was Egypt, so we entered this word into the search dialogue box and the following results appeared.

British Pathe search results

Clicking on the movie thumbnail on the left shows a selection of stills from the movie. Once we found a film we liked, we used the drop-down menu on the right to select the resolution required (in this case, Web Publishing) before clicking Add to Basket.

We continued until we had chosen a selection of movies – remember that these are fairly large downloads so you might want to choose two or three films in advance for your class rather than letting them loose on the computer at this stage. Click on Basket at the top to download the movies.

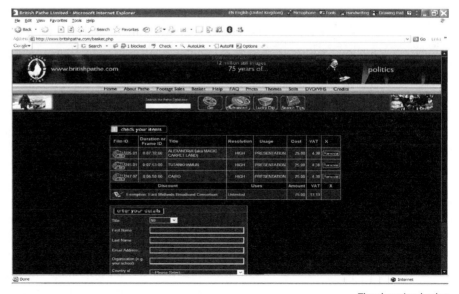

The shopping basket

Note that it would have cost £75 to buy these films commercially, but because we were doing this from a National Education Network broadband connection they were free. We filled in the form so that our receipt could be emailed to us before clicking Proceed.

To get our movies we selected the Click here to get your files link (wait a few seconds before doing this because clicking too soon may result in an error message). Save each file onto your hard disk.

For this project we wanted to use Windows Media (.wmv) versions, but if you are using a Mac choose QT6 (Quicktime 6.0). Save each file, making sure you remember where you have saved them.

Step 2

WEBSITE

The next stage is to launch Windows Movie Maker from the PC – if you don't have it on your computer, you can download it free from the Microsoft website at www.microsoft.com. We imported the movie footage by clicking Import video from the 1. Capture Video menu, repeating for all the movies downloaded from the British Pathe website.

Importing the movies into Windows Movie Maker

Windows Movie Maker automatically sliced the movie into individual scenes for us. This allowed us to choose the sections we wanted and to put them in the order required. We could watch each small clip by double-clicking it. Learners started working out an order for their storyboard and planned the text they wanted to put with it.

Pupils dragged and dropped the clips they wanted down onto the storyboard at the bottom of the screen. The result was a few clips in the order required. Using clips from several Pathe newsreels together can be interesting – taking a theme and looking at newsreels ten years apart is fascinating.

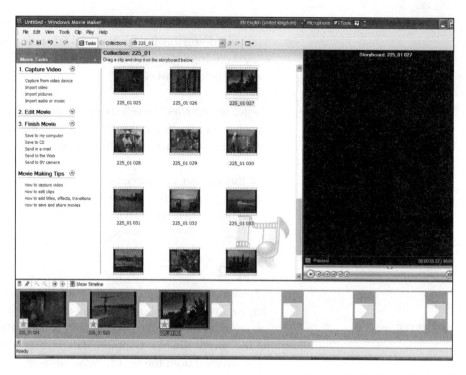

The Windows Movie Maker storyboard

Before finishing, learners added text on top using the Make titles or credits function from the 2. Edit Movie menu. These can be inserted as text between clips or on top of them. The work was saved when everyone was happy with it. It could be sent by Bluetooth over the phone to show parents at home, or a high resolution version could be shown on the whiteboard to the class or to the whole school during assembly.

This project could be adapted as follows:

➡ Quick and easy film-making: ask learners to make a short film using stock video clips and MP3 files.

➡ News programme: ask learners to take a 30-second sequence from a newsreel and then prepare and script the studio sequence before and after, perhaps role-playing an interview with an expert.

➡ Video poetry: use titling to add text to a movie.

WEBSITE

Although we used the British Pathe website, there are other excellent alternative sources for video footage you could try: the BBC Motion Gallery at www.bbc.motiongallery.com is certainly worth a look.

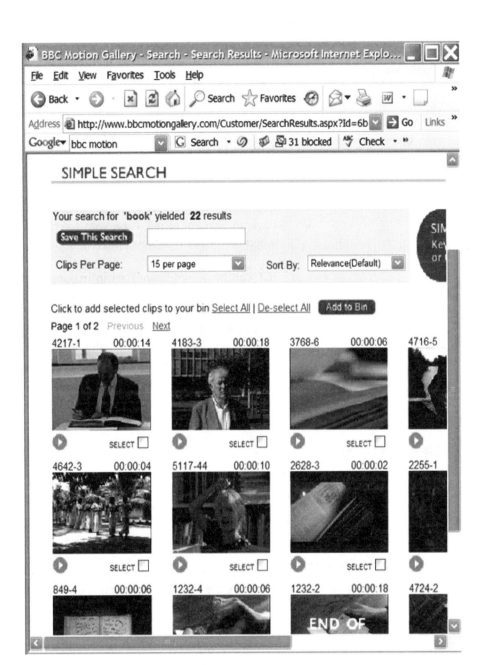

The BBC Motion Gallery website

Tools

- Broadband connection to the National Education Network.
- Windows Movie Maker.

KEY Points

- Build a repertoire of sources for images, movies and audio files that you know and can point learners to – a number are listed in this chapter.
- Find and use some of the free tools so that you feel confident with them, such as Photo Story 3, Audacity and Windows Movie Maker.
- The process of rehearsing is valuable and not lost time.
- Creative multimedia doesn't have to employ lots of complex devices.

Further activities

▌Interviews

A 'real time', face-to-face opportunity for learners to see, hear and interact with people as a resource, interviews are a good opportunity to get creative thoughts happening. They can be difficult to set up, they rarely go as planned, and they have an element of risk even with the most compliant and willing visitor, but when they work interviews provoke a huge range of ideas.

ICT can be a significant tool in making interviews work. You want to make every second of the interview count and draw out as much as you can from every learner in your class. ICT allows you to record and reproduce these details. Pupils also need to be able to express what happened with as much room as possible for them to really understand the material they are looking at. ICT allows them to select the relevant parts, bring together different sources and place them side by side quickly and easily.

Top tips

Good interviews

➡ Plan questions in advance.

➡ Be clear what is meant by each question.

➡ Use open questions for detailed answers.

➡ Use closed questions for short, precise answers.

➡ Avoid leading questions.

➡ Make the right impression with eye contact, nods, smiles and by showing respect.

You don't want pupils to spend too much of their time reading from bits of paper and scribbling down notes they might not be able to decipher anyway. If a learner's main task is scribing, they may not do much more than that. If their main task is reading each question in turn from a script, they are probably reading the next question when they should be listening to the previous answer. However, sound recording is a hugely underused ICT tool – simple, powerful and free!

Learners can rehearse questions with a microphone, recording them, playing them back, and discussing each point in turn. The microphone is potentially more democratic than the pen – it can be shared more easily and it frees people from trying to write down the first idea they thought of and then not wanting to spoil the page by altering it. The idea that early versions can be improved and that pupils will arrive at a better idea if they work at it is intrinsic to the process.

Of course, interviews can also be recorded. This will never capture every nuance, but it acts as a much more live and vibrant reminder for memories than written notes, and pupils won't miss any answers if they record the interviewee.

Top tips

Microphones and recording techniques

➡ Don't be put off by technical details about what types of microphone to use. There are some simple rules of thumb that you can manage no matter how uncomfortable you may be with the technology.

➡ The best microphone for any piece of work is the one you have! If you have a laptop, you have a microphone built in and this will work. If you have a desktop PC, it probably came with a cheap plastic one. Remember that this is just an interview – seize the moment!

➡ All kinds of things can record sound. If you don't have a microphone:

   ➡ see if your phone has a sound recorder;

   ➡ use a cassette player for now and worry about how to record to your computer later (this may not be necessary);

   ➡ see if your MP3 player can record;

   ➡ a small camcorder can make a good audio recorder if you leave the lens cap on;

   ➡ try plugging headphones into the microphone socket. It may look stupid, but it does work sometimes.

➡ Make sure learners practise well beforehand. Include at least one 'dry run' for the real thing, with someone standing in as the visitor.

➡ Don't move the microphone during the interview, and just record the subject. You can always re-record the questions later if they are unclear, but you may not need them anyway.

➡ Ask pupils to practise with different angles and distances between the microphone and the interviewee. You are aiming for something that doesn't sound distorted and doesn't need to be cranked up to full volume to be heard in playback.

➡ The biggest problem with sound at interviews isn't cheap microphones – it's background noise. Get your learners to practise in the environment as it will be set up on the day and agree how they will manage this.

Rehearsing may take a lot of time, but the process of preparing for the interview is just as important as the event itself. It will make the group less nervous, allow them to know what they are going to say much better, worry less if they don't follow the script exactly and sort out any technical glitches in advance – a good piece of learning in itself.

When your group has finished the interview, they will end up with a long sound file containing the bits you want and other things that after a few playbacks may be unnecessary. Whichever tool you use from the ones suggested below, the best approach is to ask learners to break the long file into small, single answers or sections. This has the advantages of making the finished product manageable as long media files are impractical, and giving learners a simple but relevant task to do as they begin to assimilate what happened. The process varies according to the software you are using, but essentially it works as follows:

➡ As a group, review the whole recording, making notes of the time it took and what happened.

➡ Each learner should take time to consider what they think are the most useful and interesting parts of the interview.

➡ As a group, agree a manageable number of sound clips they want to end up with, and agree which ones they should be.

➡ Go through the sound recording using the mouse to select the relevant clips, copying and pasting them into a new empty file. This file is then saved and kept in a folder for the interview. Headphones are best worn for this as it can take a while and requires persistence and patience.

➡ If required, re-record any questions to go with each extracted clip.

➡ Copy and paste the responses to the end of the questions.

If the sound has been recorded on tape, each stage diminishes the quality of the recording. However, if recorded digitally, the sound clips stay as good as the original recording or better.

Editing sound with Audacity

Audacity is a piece of free software that enables you to record and edit sound files. To download this program, visit the Audacity website at www.audacity.sourceforge.net. A link to the current version of this software can be found on the accompanying CD-ROM.

**WEBSITE
CD-ROM**

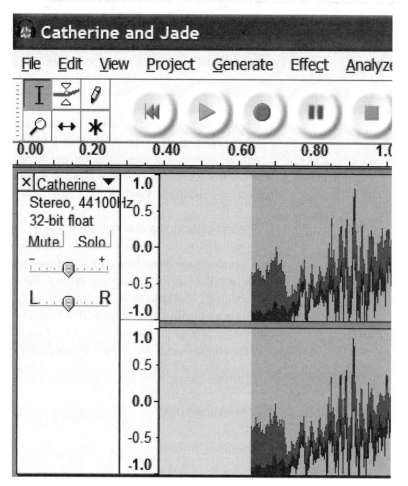

Audacity allows you to choose sound clips using your mouse and before working on them

A common problem is trying to get rid of a section either before or after the part you are interested in. To do this, try one of the following techniques:

➡ To get rid of something before the section you want, choose it and then use Edit, Delete or Edit, Silence (which leaves the time in but reduces the noise to nothing).

➡ To keep only the part you are interested in, select it and then click on Edit, Trim.

If the sound levels seem low, you can boost them with Effect, Amplify. Try increasing the amplitude in small steps of 0.2dB or so. This also amplifies background noise and hiss, so if your recording is too quiet in the first place it won't solve everything.

Most of the effects in the Generate menu are good for music but useless for interviews.

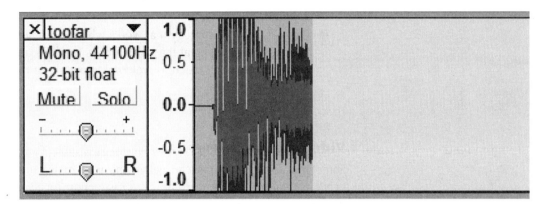

The input levels are too high and the result will be a distorted or 'clipped' sound file – move the microphone away from the subject

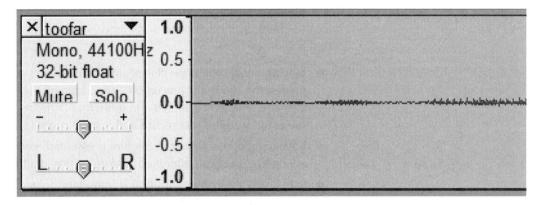

The difference between the peak levels of sound and the background noise is too low – either move the microphone nearer, ask the subject to speak louder or reduce background noise

▌Taking photos during interviews

Digital cameras add visuals to the piece that learners will produce afterwards, and in movie-making mode they can capture a snippet of the subject that will make a good whole-class resource. However, taking photos isn't the primary activity and should not derail the interview itself:

➡ Learners need to be up-front about taking photos and offer the interviewee the chance to decline. This request should figure in their rehearsal. If the subject is under 16 years of age, permission might be needed from a parent or carer.

➡ Just as the group has rehearsed other aspects of the interview, the person taking photos ought to ensure they know how to use the camera and have a plan of the photos they intend to take.

➡ The subject may feel more comfortable posing for a photograph than having it taken while answering a question. Be prepared to take two or three photos and then put the camera away.

➡ There are only so many photos of 'interviewee talking to pupils' that your group will need. Perhaps they could think about taking some closer shots as an alternative to repeating the same one time and again. Try focusing the camera on the subject's face, hands or shoes – smaller details that might fit the responses.

➡ It is better to switch off the flash unless the interviews are happening in a dark room.

➡ One group-work strategy that works when you have a number of interviewees arriving at the same time is for the learners to take charge of different aspects, such as welcoming people or taking photos on behalf of the class.

Videoing interviews

Sometimes video cameras can get in the way of learning, as meeting their needs for cables and power can be a distraction for everyone. Just because videos are more 'high gloss', this doesn't mean they will add a great deal to the group's understanding of what was said. They might even reduce the benefits of bringing ICT into the project in the first place.

There are times, however, when it may be appropriate to use camcorders. The principles behind microphones and cameras apply just as much to videos, sound and image work:

➡ Moving a video recorder during an interview isn't recommended. We suggest the camera is placed on a tripod facing the subject, ideally at their eye level when seated and more than a metre away. Once the subject is seated, press record and leave it running.

➡ If having the interviewer in the film is essential, you could record them asking the questions afterwards before editing it all together.

➡ Rehearsing the camera position is important if you plan to use the audio from it as your main record of the session. Microphones in video cameras are more susceptible to background noise and struggle to get clear sound when the subject isn't facing them directly. Therefore, you need to have greater control of the interview environment to make it work well in the medium of video.

An approach where a small amount of video is used to enhance an interview rather than being the main event can be very rewarding. Camera phones and digital cameras can be used to grab a short sequence within an interview. This can be used in a presentation or another piece of work produced from it, while the audio material remains the main record.

Top tips

Outside-in sessions

➡ Getting ready for an interview isn't a problem – it's part of the solution!

➡ By rehearsing, learners not only get better at doing the activity, they also free themselves to get more from the activity itself.

➡ Research as a social activity that helps to make that 'leap of understanding'.

➡ Make sharing equipment a positive impact by the way you set the activity up.

➡ Make web-based work 'sticky' (see pages 98–99) by forcing an outcome that needs some mental processing.

➡ Services like broadband offer much more than simple web-research – look for resources and team them with active learning activities.

➡ 'Old' technology such as audio cassette recorders can do the job just as well – don't be lured into wasting time with technology.

▌ Framing shots

	Near	**Far**
Wide angle (zoom out)	Audio should be good and we can see some background such as the interviewer. The subject may find themselves looking at the camera almost instinctively.	Watch out for poor-quality audio as background noise might confuse your camera, but the subject is perhaps less conscious of the camera.
Telephoto (zoom in)	Audio should be fairly good and you will get an excellent recording of facial expressions, but watch out for the subject moving out of shot while talking – by leaning back, for example.	Watch out for poor-quality audio as background noise might confuse your camera, but this is a good compromise in quieter settings.

Using a webcam and OneNote

Our day-to-day work involves interviewing learners and teachers and at various times we have used the approaches described in this chapter. Recently we have hit on another method that is simpler, although the quality of results can be hit and miss.

For this activity, you will need a basic webcam. Light to carry, it can be plugged into your PC or laptop for low quality video and audio recording with little hassle. You will also need a piece of software called Microsoft OneNote. This program isn't expensive for educational use and for note-taking it's an absolute top-rate program. The best trick OneNote has is that if you record audio or video while you are typing notes it synchronizes the video with the written notes. So each time you hit the return key on the keyboard, you have 'sliced' the video neatly.

Picture the scene: a laptop with OneNote and a webcam, the interviewer simply hits return when they start to ask a question, and again when the answer starts, and they end up with a short, neat clip for each. For minimal outlay you have a set-up that makes interviewing a simple day-to-day event.

Web-based creative research

We know the web can lead to learning-free teaching, but it's an opportunity to bring the outside world into the classroom with minimal effort. In this activity, we will think about how to use the web as an alternative to real people and objects – as a research tool.

Also known as 'Google learning', friction-free learning is based on how a tool is used, not the merits of the tool itself. Consider the task 'research Ancient Egypt over the next 30 minutes'. What often happens is that pupils search the web using Google, perhaps ticking all kinds of ICT skills boxes by formulating searches correctly, finding material and printing it. They are essentially playing a game – and you win the game when you put stuff into your folder. They aim to 'win' with as little effort as possible – it isn't uncommon to have a group of pupils spending any amount of time you like with no learning happening whatsoever. This is the opposite of what we aim to achieve with web-based research.

What we have to do to make using the web a creative tool is to make it 'sticky' – to come up with ways to make the 'game' one where reading, thinking about and responding to ideas is how learners win. Most strategies for 'sticky' learning are common-sense approaches that have worked with printed resources for years, but too often when we go digital we have to go back to basics to remind ourselves of good practice.

For example, copying from a text or worksheet has largely been discredited as a useful thing to do, but in the Industrial Age copying text accurately was actually a useful skill – the clerical worker being the information system of the age – and so it was encouraged. In the Information Age we have machines that do this for us, so tasks need to make learners respond to material.

Talking through a web page or resource can be a useful activity – just as you would work as a group with a class reader, projectors allow a class to focus on a well-chosen online source in much the same way. Reading aloud, questioning, highlighting on-screen and copying selected parts to a document shared and developed by everyone can make everyday use of interactive whiteboards.

'Sticky' learning activities

➡ 'Using information found on the web, write a newspaper article.'

➡ 'Find three web pages that support your argument about this topic and highlight the key sentences.'

➡ 'A new pupil is doing research on this topic. Write a short guide to the sites she should read and explain why.'

➡ 'Find two sites on the web about this topic and find out who made each one. Which site do you think is more reliable and useful? Explain why.'

➡ 'Find a web page about this topic in French/German/Spanish. Use a web-based translation tool to convert it to English and then go through the text to improve it until it reads like it was written originally in English.'

There seems to be an assumption that research-based ICT work is an individual activity, when actually discussion around research is often what is needed to internalize it. How you use the web depends on how ICT is set up for your classroom. We have worked on the assumption that you have only a small number of computers available, but that you can get access to more when needed either in your room or elsewhere.

The whole class on the web

Web browsing can be a tremendous social activity, and if well moderated can be useful for a whole-class activity such as a starter, plenary or transition activity. To do it well, you need your laptop or PC to plug in to a set of speakers and projector, or you could use the speaker built into most projectors – perfectly acceptable for low-volume work. All kinds of set-ups can be useful, ranging from interactive whiteboards, wireless projectors and Tablet PCs, to a simple wireless mouse passed from learner to learner. The key is that only one person controls what is on the screen all the time (this could be a pupil) and that the really interesting part is the response to the web-based material, not the pages themselves. Too often we end up surfing while pupils watch, which doesn't make best use of our skills or engage learners.

➡ Once you have established what you are looking for, search for material. Even if you know where you want to end up, you need to model the process of finding it to reinforce these skills for learners. Whether you are using a learning platform (a safe, managed set of material on the National Education Network) or the wilds of the internet through Google, Yahoo! or MSN, the process is similar. Do rehearse searches before the lesson to ensure you don't get too many surprises, and do find out how to turn on any filters against unsuitable content if they are available.

➡ The group needs to be helped to agree, to describe what they are looking for and to piece together the search terms to use. Although you may well find a perfectly good website with a single-word search, it might not be the best one for the job.

Top tips

Effective searching

➡ Always look for an 'advanced search' option. There you will have the choice of whether you are looking for a specific set of words that all have to appear, or just some, or together in a particular pattern.

➡ Go Boolean! When you want two words to both appear in a web page, use the + sign. For example, if you want the page to contain the words 'pyramid' and 'worker', enter 'pyramid + worker'.

➡ Alternatively, try using OR. For example, if the page should contain the words 'pyramid' or 'worker', enter 'pyramid OR worker' – this may give very different results!

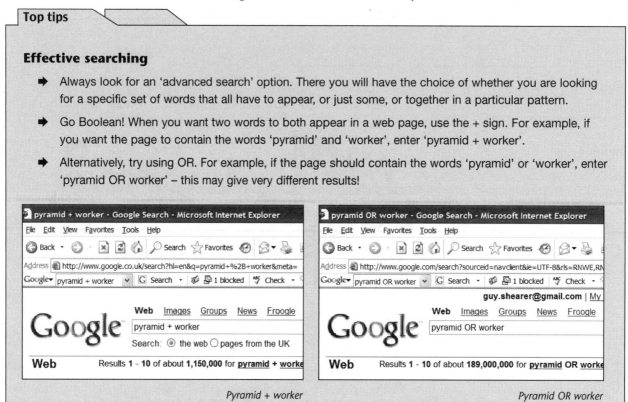

Pyramid + worker   Pyramid OR worker

➡ Take time to look through the pages offered for your search and talk about them a little before diving in. Key questions are 'Who made this site and what do they know about this subject?' and 'Can I trust this site as a source of information?'.

➡ Make a note of any pages you want to visit for later, perhaps using the Favorites option.

➡ Remember to help the group browse the content of the page quickly. Scrolling down could be a problem unless you manage it because the person with control of the mouse will always be itching to click, click, click.

➡ Have a routine where you ask the group to pause for, say, 30 seconds in silence before beginning. This works well, especially when followed by asking for keywords or key questions from the group. Use an interactive whiteboard, which allows those points to be displayed.

➡ Begin to ask questions. Ask learners to read out key passages or take control of the mouse to mark them.

➡ Group activities belong to the group – find ways of sharing the work they all put in rather than asking them to repeat it again later when alone. You could try asking the person in control of the mouse to copy and paste content into a word-processing document for you to print and put on the notice board or to save in a shared space on your school network.

Top tips

Managing your favourites

➡ First create a folder in which to hold your favourites. Choose Favorites from the menu, then Organize Favorites. Click on Create Folder and enter an appropriate title for the folder.

➡ Go to the website you want to store and choose Favorites, Add to Favorites. Click the Create in button and find your folder, then choose OK.

➡ Train your class to do this if you all share one or two PCs.

Group-work on the web

Group-work and computers can be a problem. Asking pupils to share computers is an almost inevitable situation in many classrooms, but ICT offers so much more in terms of the benefits we can get from it. One or two people in the group are able to engage with the ICT part of the activity a bit, but really engage themselves with thinking and understanding. This means we need to set up the group-work situation right from the outset with this in mind.

It is much easier if your learners are used to working as a whole class, talking and thinking about web content rather than randomly scrolling through it without any ideas coming to them. Strategies that work include the following:

➡ Assign clear roles within the group and use those roles enough times for the class to get used to them. Have a 'driver' whose main job is using the PC; a 'navigator' whose main job is to summarize quickly what is on the page and draw everyone's attention to the key sections; a 'recorder' whose main job is to synthesize the most important results, what gets kept for the final piece of work, and what gets saved and printed.

➡ Rotate people through the roles – allow pupils to decide for themselves within parameters you have set.

➡ Give praise to all the roles equally and make your assessment weigh between all three so nobody feels they might lose the 'game' by playing in a poor position.

➡ Don't swap roles during an activity – let the group get into role and keep with it until the task is finished.

➡ Go for well-defined aims for the group and well-defined time targets. Questions that require understanding rather than finding facts work best, such as 'What things would an ancient Egyptian pyramid builder have been most worried about?'.

Working alone on the web

Working alone productively on the web can be harder than with company, although it's seen traditionally as something done on your own. When learners have to do web research by themselves, there should be a good reason for it, and even then they might want to have a partner to help them take notes and keep to task. Solo work can make for good reinforcement when linked to concrete, fact-based tasks, such as 'What did Egyptian pyramid builders eat on special occasions?'.

A key part of planning for working alone on the web is to have a really clear expected outcome: what are pupils going to do as a result of the session? This outcome may not be as open-ended or reflective as a group-work situation, although there are always some individuals who can manage well. If you keep to 'sticky' learning and make the outcome clear, you will have set them up with a good chance to succeed.

Top tips

Things to avoid

➡ Make sure you sort out cables and wires in advance to avoid wasting time – ask a learner to take over and face the class if necessary!

➡ Be sure pupils agree about who does what before the interviewee arrives.

➡ Don't let an interview take place if at the end all you have are some handwritten notes.

➡ Brief pupils on what is required – projects handed in with clipart and text are lacking in real digital content.

➡ Don't let learners sit for ages browsing the internet without any outcome.

➡ Look out for printouts with website addresses on the footer – if they have been printed straight from the internet, they have probably not been read!

➡ Avoid arguments about whose turn it is to use the mouse.

▌ Webquests

Webquests are structured approaches to using the internet with learners in a way that appeals to them. They can be a social activity as well as a solo one; they can work well in a classroom situation as well as outside the school.

Webquests are student-centred and enquiry-based challenges that require learners to explore the web for information. They include any links that are appropriate for learners to research, as well as suggestions for further research. Generally, they comprise an introduction, a process, a task, a list of resources, a conclusion and an evaluation.

This means that you have to prepare webquests, much as you would prepare a worksheet, or use someone else's. Luckily, the tools are easy to use and readily available providing you focus on the learning rather than the technology.

WEBSITE

As webquests are remarkably popular in the USA, many are available on the internet. If you look at those available on a popular site, such as Best WebQuests at www.bestwebquests.com, you might be put off by the unfamiliar curriculum references. However, select one that matches a topic you are covering and give it a go as a supplementary activity. Seeing which parts the learners get the most out of will help you build your own webquests.

Making your own webquests

There are some online tools for building webquests, and many are free. Perhaps the easiest, simplest approach is to use either Word or PowerPoint, whichever you are most comfortable with. Once you have decided on the purpose of the quest, simply fill in the blanks on the template:

➡ The big question: one or two sentences telling learners what they have to achieve as an outcome.

➡ Role pages: break the bigger research areas into a number of specialist areas for each member of the group to get their teeth into. Find three or four good website starting points for each and put links on the page for them to follow.

➡ Group task: outline the specific thing learners need to do together after they have completed their individual tasks – perhaps a report, a presentation or a drama piece.

➡ Scoring page: give a one-sentence description for whatever levels you want to assign to the task in a form that allows the group to evaluate themselves objectively.

▌ Digitizing materials

An object or analogue recording, such as a printed page or old film, can be a powerful and inspiring stimulus. ICT allows us to keep these objects beyond the time we can afford to store them, to enlarge them, to view them from any angle, to make limitless perfect copies and to take them home.

Digitizing artefacts doesn't have to be hard work – just like interviews, the work of preparing and setting up is valuable in itself, developing ICT and interpersonal skills and bringing pupils intimately and purposefully into contact with the artefact.

Artefacts

There are two ways that objects brought into your classroom can be better used through ICT:

➡ Giving the whole class a quick and easy close-up view: sharing an object with the whole class is simple if you can use a projector or large screen. It doesn't replace the tactile side of working with real objects, but it does remove any anxiety to get a good view. Ways of achieving this include the following:

  ➡ If you have access to a webcam, plug it into your laptop or PC and use it to display a large, live view of the object on your wall. This feature is available with some projectors, but this approach works with any.

  ➡ If you have a camcorder, it is easier to use the video leads (or those with your projector) and to link it directly into the back of the projector. This is a good technique to give a live, close-up view. Many video cameras have a facility called macro, which allows you to get really near to a page or object for an 'extreme' close-up shot.

➡ Recording the object for future use:

  ➡ Collect a set of photos from most angles and a variety of distances and keep them together in a folder accessible to the group when needed.

  ➡ If it's relevant, use a tool like Audacity to capture some sound associated with the object.

CD-ROM

Videos

Domestic video cassette recorders don't have a long history to them, but already you could describe all kinds of footage held on them as 'historical'. Getting this footage digitized so you can keep it for future use, manipulate it, and allow your learners the freedom to use it can be a tough challenge. A number of approaches for digitizing videos are suggested below, and further information can be found on the accompanying CD-ROM.

➡ Cheap and nasty: a low-tech and rather cottage-industry approach is to hook up a VCR to your projector, black out the room, point a digital camcorder at the image and record away. You lose quality, you need silence to get good results, but it does work!

➡ Easy: if you work somewhere that employs an audiovisual technician, go and say hi! This is something they should be able to do for you. An alternative is to check whether any parents or friends of the school do this kind of thing for a hobby – you may be surprised how popular it is.

➡ Medium: if you have a digital video camera, have a look to see if it has phono-style video plugs or (more likely) a small jack socket and a cable from that ending in phono plugs. This allows you to hook a VCR output straight to the camera – play on the VCR, record on the digital video camera and you will have a digital copy to download onto the computer. If you don't know a technician, this technique is a good solution.

➡ Hard: in theory, buying a 'proper' solution ought to be easy, but our experience of using 'dazzle boxes' to convert video to digital signals is patchy. These devices, available from good electrical retailers, take a video signal in and give you a digital signal out that plugs straight into your PC.

Taking photos of objects

As well as taking photos of the whole object, another idea is to take close-up shots from different angles using the macro facility on your digital camera. Make a folder for each object and include five or six photos within it – the first being a well-lit shot of the whole object. Alternate between detail and whole-object views to make a slide show you can leave running on-screen or on a whiteboard while discussing the item, or to use as a screensaver. Allow learners to use the photos in their own outcomes to escape from some of that rather over-used clipart for a while.

Super-demonstrations

The notion of 'I'll demonstrate how to do it, then you have a go' crops up all the time. This idea came from a hair and beauty lecture (where it really is important that the perm is done correctly!), but it applies anywhere.

Use a sequence of images or movies to illustrate the key 30-second part of your demonstration (the one learners are always asking you to repeat once they are under way with the task) and leave it playing. If a learner gets stuck, all they have to do is to wait until the right part of the loop comes up again to remind them. You can make these aides-memoire easily using one of the following methods:

➡ Insert photos into a PowerPoint slide show that repeats itself, changing the slide every five seconds. A pupil could take these photos during your demo to the class and paste them into a templated slide show for you.

➡ Film the demo (or just the vital bits) with a camcorder or a webcam. Import the film into Windows Movie Maker and set it to play on a loop (again, a pupil could do this for you).

➡ If you use an interactive whiteboard, many have a record feature that allows you to convert a section of your work into a movie you can play in a loop.

● Use an iPod with a microphone or another MP3 audio unit (many cheaper ones come with an inbuilt microphone) for interviews – you don't need a computer if you just hook it back into speakers to replay to the audience. Record each answer as a separate 'track'.

● Use camera phones. The pictures can be sent to a web page using instant messaging or to a PC using Bluetooth.

● Hook your camera directly to your television/projector (most cameras come with a cable for this) or get a card viewer to allow you to play the contents of a memory card directly on a television or projector – these are cheap and available from photography shops and many mobile phone retailers.

Chapter 6

Performing

This chapter outlines ideas and practical ICT suggestions for equipment and software you can use in a multimedia context to produce resources, work projects or archives of progress and achievement in the performing arts field. Examples include video analysis and editing; adding sound, voiceovers and music tracks; and adding text.

The performing arts field is a specialist area, so we decided to include this chapter. However, relevant cross-curricular material for other subject areas is also given. The performing arts material is based on a project designed to use ICT to support the subject in specialist colleges in Northamptonshire. The activities that used ICT are video, sound and music editing; music sequencing; digital radio stations; sound and video recording of the creative performance; applying sports performance software; using video playback to enhance performance; and using dance and music notation software to notate dance steps and music.

Most creative arts subjects have three main areas – composition, performance and evaluation – and all these areas can be made more effective by the use of ICT. This isn't a way of replacing traditional skills and methods, but it is a tool that, when used appropriately and effectively, can enhance and enable creativity. People without highly developed performance skills, or with disabilities, have been enabled or given access to performance opportunities that they could not aspire to without the aid of ICT.

Performance is a fleeting moment; it happens then it instantly becomes a memory. ICT allows us to capture the moment for review, analysis or celebration of the achievement. ICT can also notate work, allowing us to write down our ideas and trial them without needing to find performers and using rehearsal time. Another possible use of ICT is to produce resources that can be customized to each performer's individual needs or situation, such as creating a setting (back projections) that set the mood or ambience, or writing specially edited music.

Technology using sound or light beams to trigger music or sounds could be used to initiate or enhance a performance. Another new development area in ICT is to use movement sensors that, when triggered, play music, video or photo extracts. These could provide stimuli for composition or improvisation in music, drama or dance. Videoconference facilities enable different groups of performers to perform simultaneously in different locations, opening up the concert venue to a wider audience. Media, video, digital radio, television and web streaming are powerful tools that can exemplify, celebrate and share performances. They can also strongly influence much wider audiences and increase the impact of the ideas and concepts contained within the performance.

These ICT activities can be adapted according to your pupils. For example:

➡ At Key Stages 1 and 2, films can be recorded using Digital Blue cameras. These can be animated and include sound effects, music and voiceovers. Digital videos and stills can be taken and provided as a stimulus. These can be used in any subject area for literacy, numeracy, science and so on. Simple music programs that have been pre-sequenced could be used. Basic webcams could be used to create videoconference links. Sounds could be recorded using Audacity before these are edited to create new sounds and compositions. The finished work could be broadcast on digital radio or web streamed.

➡ At Key Stages 3–5, music software can be used to generate and notate music. Sequencing software can be used to compose and provide backing tracks for soloists to perform to. Digital videos can be used not only to record the work process and end result, but also for analysis and to aid the review and refinement process. Videos and stills can be used to provide back projections and to create starting points or stimulus for creative work. Videoconference links allow workshops or master classes to be linked between locations or as a conference meeting for teachers to moderate exam work from individual centres.

➡ For special needs learners, audio or voiceovers can aid understanding and access to materials for the visually impaired. Text subtitles on film can help the hearing impaired to understand and access information more effectively. Switches can help those with physical disabilities and restricted movement to access computers and technical equipment. Music sequencing software with pre-recorded tracks allows less-gifted musicians to compose and produce compositions with a professional feel.

Multimedia is becoming increasingly important in producing resources and archiving evidence of achievement. It is also important as a vehicle for learners to investigate, show understanding and record achievement. Performing arts function well without using ICT, but technology allows learners to improve the quality of their work. ICT is an enabling tool that allows us to work more efficiently and opens up new possibilities, whether through performance, review, analysis, investigation or archiving. ICT has taken composition and performance to new audiences and provided access for those with disabilities. It can act not only as an 'equalizer' to allow those less gifted the opportunity to participate and to experience the enjoyment of performing and being creative, but also as a facilitator to allow us to achieve a greater level of expertise.

ICT to enhance performance

A class of Key Stage 4 performing arts students from Latimer Arts College was working in groups of four on a drama based around a number of themes including the pressure from peers to try drugs. One group set the scene in a nightclub where one person was to be intimidated into trying drugs by a number of friends. They decided the ideal medium in which to develop and present their drama would be a video clip.

WEBSITE

The starting point was to create a film backdrop, projected onto a large screen to create atmosphere and mood. Students did this by downloading video clips from the BBC Motion Gallery website at www.bbcmotiongallery.com, which contains a large number of clips that are small in size for quick downloads. They then extracted the audio from the video files and imported them into Audacity. They then distorted the music and amplified the bass to create the sort of music and sound you would experience in a nightclub setting. The music and videos were then played and projected onto the background screen while pupils acted out their scripted performance in front of the screen. This was filmed on digital video cameras. Pupils also did an improvised version of their drama, which was also filmed.

When all the filming was complete, pupils downloaded their video onto computers, editing the clips to produce a final film. This was then saved as a video file, which could be either shown or archived as portfolio evidence of their drama work.

- Digital camera.
- Tripod.
- Specialist software for the area.
- General-purpose software, such as Audacity, Photo Story 3 and Movie Maker.

- ICT can improve performance by adding new media.
- ICT can improve performing by supporting review and experimentation.

Further activities

Videos

Video is an efficient way of capturing the creative process and the end result, or the performance itself. It can be used effectively in many subject areas, but it is a particularly powerful tool in performing arts subjects such as music, drama and dance.

Music

Video can be used in instrumental lessons and for performances. Learners can study performance techniques such as embouchure, hand/arm position, stance and bowing methods. The video can be watched, analysed and discussed. You could be filmed demonstrating the correct technique and pupils can watch and retain the video for future reference.

Video can be used in music performances

Larger groups of musicians could be videoed, particularly when working on ensemble technique. Learners take time to develop a feel for or sense of ensemble – an awareness of what other musicians are doing and making minor adjustments to play in time and match the dynamics, style and mood of the performance. By watching their ensemble performances, learners can see who isn't responding, what skills they lack and note when others get it right. The ensemble is working as a team, watching each other, listening and anticipating changes, rather than waiting for them to happen then reacting later.

Class performances and concerts can also be videoed. Reflecting and analysing the performance provides pointers for future improvements and developments. It also provides evidence of achievement, progress and celebration.

Video can also be used as a composition stimulus, either as a concept or as a resource to which a music soundtrack can be composed and added.

Drama

Videos can be a record of work progress from stimulus to finished performance. They can be filmed from different perspectives or provide a backdrop to improvise or act with. Film techniques are different from stage acting, so video also provides the opportunity to explore different acting techniques such as close-ups, subtle expressions and gestures with the opportunity for learners to see and receive instant feedback.

Video can be used to film individual or group performances. You can film from multiple locations, giving a different perspective to the work. It can provide a record of the creative work process.

As in music, video can also facilitate reflection and analysis of the drama performance, but its greatest advantage is that it can be revisited at a later date and referred back to without losing any detail. Video analysis provides pointers for future improvement and development, while also providing evidence of achievement, progress and celebration.

Dance

Video is an excellent tool for analysing dance technique. Dance movements can be subtle but quick and often the human eye misses small details. Video allows you to play back frame by frame or at a slower speed to check for symmetry, extension, stance and so on. If you are working with a group of dancers, the ensemble can be checked to give you an overall picture.

Video allows playback to analyse dance movements

Dancers cover a lot of space, making it difficult to capture performances, so you need to consider what aspects you wish to film and how many cameras you need. Unlike with music, ensuring sound quality isn't critical. One camera on a tripod can be used effectively to view the performance from one angle or audience perspective. Alternatively, you could set the camera on the tripod and follow individuals or zoom in and out during filming. You could also move around the room while filming, but this is far more difficult to do well – particularly with small digital cameras – and should be avoided. If you set up a number of cameras, think about the angles and view through the camera eyepiece or screen: what you see is what you get!

Across the curriculum

Video can be used in all subject areas to record the work process or as a medium for learners to express themselves or their understanding of a concept or idea:

➡ Investigations: learners could undertake an investigation and film the process. Examples include making a documentary about gravity, why earthquakes happen or what is photosynthesis. Alternatively, they could re-enact a historical event.

➡ Record sports events: video can be used to record events, field trips, visits, videoconferenced meetings or interviews and stored for future reference. It is particularly useful in recording sporting achievements, where video analysis linked to relevant feedback leads to future aims and appropriate training programmes.

➡ Record the process (design and technology, art): a video or series of stills can record work in progress. Subjects such as design and technology and art work through a process: concept, design and production of the article. A series of photos can form a record of this process. Much can be learned by watching an expert demonstrate a creative process, which is then recorded on video, edited into stages and retained to show to learners. If web streamed, stored on disk or saved online, it can be accessible to a wider audience of learners.

➡ Unravelling to create: video can be useful to analyse or take a story or concept apart before being re-created or retold in another way. This reinforces the work and shows that it is understood. Making a video can be the medium for this, as well as being a useful record of the learners' thought processes and progress.

Top tips

Videos

➡ When recording music performances, use good-quality external microphones that have been strategically placed.

➡ Place a few cameras at different locations to get different angle shots.

➡ Use a tripod – this gives clearer shots and avoids camera shake.

➡ Check light levels and set the white balance on the camera. Filming in dark or bright rooms affects the picture quality, so you need to set up the camera as accurately as possible. Adjust the lighting as appropriate and close the curtains or blinds.

➡ If cameras are pre-set and left to run automatically, check they capture the full range of movement.

➡ If you use the cameras' internal microphones, check the sound levels are set correctly and that the microphones are turned on.

➡ Look through the eyepiece or at the screen. Remember that what you see is what you get!

➡ Label the tapes. There is nothing worse than looking through a batch of unmarked tapes and having to view each one. Get into the habit of dating and labelling them, preferably before you put it into the camera.

➡ Digital recordings can be downloaded straight onto a computer to view and edit.

Storage and editing

Once you have made your film, you could simply review it and then store the tape away, dated and labelled, but this isn't the most effective use of tape, which can deteriorate with time. Small tapes are also easy to lose, damage and store.

If you download the footage, the tape could be reused – making economic sense. You can store the footage and it's available for editing and broadcasting.

When you have completed downloading and editing the film, you can store it back on the original tape, save it on your hard drive (remember that film requires massive storage and will use up a lot of the hard disk space), save it to an external hard drive, or burn it onto a CD or DVD.

If you have an older camera that uses analogue tape, convert the tape to digital by playing it through a conversion device called a 'dazzle box'. These are available from good electrical retailers and you will be able to save the digital file to your computer, where you can either edit it or burn it to disk.

CD-ROM

If you want to edit your video and have Windows XP, you can use Movie Maker, a free video-editing program. Microsoft provides free online updates and downloads, together with ideas to enhance your editing and creative projects. More information on using Movie Maker is available on the accompanying CD-ROM.

If you have a Mac, you can use iMovie. Both programs are good entry-level video-editing packages. Other programs available are Roxio VideoWave Movie Creator, Ulead VideoStudio and Pinnacle Studio. At the top end of the market and suitable for professional editing is Adobe Premiere Pro and, for Macs, Final Cut Express.

You may need to edit your videos because you have extensive footage that isn't required, or you simply want to keep small extracts. Maybe you wish to edit out mistakes or change the order of the events or performances. Compilations of a performer's work over a period of time could provide a portfolio. You could add subtitles to mark each section, to date the film, or to identify a piece of work or performer.

With video editing you can cut out or move sections and paste them together, as well as rearranging clips into any order. You can trim off the beginning or end of small clips. You can join scenes with transition effects to give a professional feel to the film. You can add special effects, narration, sound effects or music. You can add titles or text to the film or provide a written commentary allow hearing-impaired people to access the video.

Video analysis

Video allows us to replay performances, study them, pause at any point and replay scenes. It also allows us to come back to a performance at a time that suits us and as often as we wish. We can use video to analyse the performance visually and aurally, noting any good and bad points or ideas for improvement or comparison. We can video different performers (including teachers or professionals) using the same piece of equipment and show them to students to compare techniques.

In recent years, performance software has been developed, mainly for the professional sports industry. Gradually the importance of this type of software is being recognized in performing arts and it's being used to analyse music, dance and drama performances. You start by creating a 'button' named after a specific move, dance step or technicality – whatever specific point you wish to examine or compare. You then play the video tape and click on the appropriately named button every time you see that technique in the video, continuing throughout the film. When you have completed this process, work with the short clips linked to the buttons. The software allows you to play two clips side by side or to overlay two clips, one on top of the other. For example, imagine you are studying a dancer's turns to the left and right for symmetry. You could overlay them onto those of a professional or play them side by side for comparison. This data could be edited together and given to the pupil for feedback.

WEBSITE

Another product on the market is SportsCode Gamebreaker from Sportstec (www.sportstec.com). This is a digital video analysis system that can be used for sport, music, drama, dance, art, design and technology or anything else where you wish to analyse a process or performance.

Stills

Still photos can be used to capture a moment or record an occasion. They can also be taken using a fast shutter speed, which can be animated into a film, or a slow shutter speed, which gives special effects. Stills can be displayed in a photo gallery created using PowerPoint on a PC, Apple iPhoto on a Mac or an iPod. You could also make a collage of photos to play on a plasma screen to greet visitors, celebrate an event or as a display area to show work. Photos could also be taken, edited and used as a backdrop or stimulus for a composition, dance or drama. They make a great back projection to display behind performers, enhancing the performance or triggering innovative improvisations – particularly if linked to a musical extract. Although colour photography tends to be the norm, black and white photos can be very dramatic and evocative. Photos can also be used to record a slow process, such as plants growing. Photograph everything in the same position every day or at set intervals, then animate them or insert them into a PowerPoint slide show and you can see the plant growing.

Recording text, audio and making notes

Using ICT to record data can be efficient and easy to retrieve. PDAs are small, portable devices that can record audio (for example, commentaries, lectures, meetings and tutorials) as well as allowing you to write notes. These can be saved, retrieved and Bluetoothed to another device such as a computer before being stored with other data and records. This is a convenient way to record and save observations and comments while watching a rehearsal or during any type of practical assessment, without having to take your eyes off the performer.

WEBSITE

Many mobile phones have similar facilities to a PDA, so try using your phone to record and download data. iPods are not just for playing music: you can buy an iTalk voice recorder from the Griffin Technology website at www.griffintechnology.com, which you either plug into the iPod or use as a clip-on lapel mike.

Tablet PCs are useful portable computers that can be used to record sound and play back film and photos, as well as allowing you to write with them.

Photo viewers

A photo viewer

The low-cost gadget above is a photo viewer. It takes memory cards from cameras or other sources and plays any pictures it finds on them through a standard video out plug fed into a television, video recorder or projector. The remote control allows you to scan forwards and backwards through the pictures, to rotate them by 90° left or right, and to start a slide show. The process of getting images from the card onto the screen takes seconds if you spend a short time beforehand making sure you have it wired correctly to the television.

The potential is massive – there is no waiting for compelling and useful feedback, stimulus and praise, and there is none of the complexity of a PC.

Enhance your plenaries with a near-instant set of images from the activity, which can be linked into the class question-and-answer session simply by asking 'What was happening when this photo was taken?', 'What do you call this type of apparatus?' or 'What is wrong here?'.

Specialist notation software

Music sequencing and notation software has been a developing industry for some time. There are many free products available alongside professional software designed for different age groups and levels. Most of these products allow you to write out music scores and play back what you have written. You can print out your completed score or save it to disk. Dance notation software also exists and is designed to be used by choreographers to record dance steps. Both are highly successful products worth investigating.

Music sequencing software

Music sequencing software has developed rapidly in recent years. Sequenced, looped and sampled music has developed its own genre and many people are building a successful career as an exponent of this. It is certainly one of the ICT products that enables less-skilled musicians to produce professional, multi-tracked compositions.

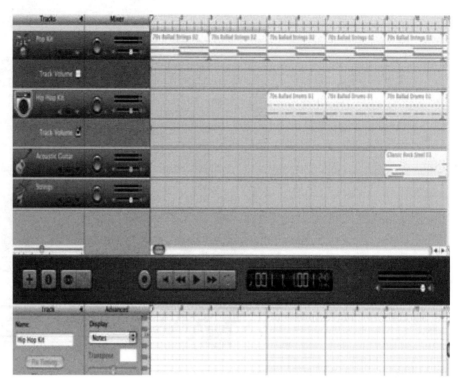

Apple GarageBand music sequencing software

Midi keyboard linked to a computer with Cubase sequencing software

Music notation software

Music notation software enables you to play live (via keyboard, guitar or pick up) in 'real time' and record directly to the computer, which notates the music. Alternatively, you can input each note individually. This type of software also allows you to add lyrics and dynamics before playing them back and listening to the notated music. You can continually edit the instrumental and vocal parts, and set them out as a full score before printing or burning to disk. Sibelius (www.sibelius.com) has recently released version 4, which allows you to copy and paste a selected passage of music to the clipboard, so that it can be pasted into other applications.

WEBSITE

Selecting

Before you can **edit** anything, you must **select** it. Selected items become **blue** (or green if in voice 2 on a stave, etc).

*   To select a note, **click on the note head.**

*   To select all the notes in a bar, **click within the bar**, away from any notes or rests.

*   To select all the bars in one line of music, **double click any bar** on the line.

*   To select all the bars in the piece for one instrument, **triple click any bar.**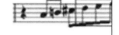

*   To select **consecutive** notes, **draw a selection box** round the notes you want.

*   To select several notes which are **not** consecutive, hold down **Ctrl** and click on the notes one at a time.

*   To select several consecutive bars in one instrument, **either** draw a selection box round the bars you want **or** (1) **click the first bar** you want, then (2) **Shift+click the last bar** you want:

*   To select several consecutive bars in a number of instruments which are above each other, **either** draw a selection box round the bars you want **or** (1) **click the first bar** of the passage in the **top stave**, then (2) **Shift+click the last bar** of the passage in the **bottom stave.**

A blue rectangle will surround the selection. Now anything which you do to one note (e.g. add an

accent) will be done to all notes in all staves within the selection.

Sibelius music notation software

Dance notation software

There are a number of dance notation packages on the market – some of them free – which allow choreographers to notate dance sequences and archive them.

TASK 6 Make floor plans

A. Select Floor Plan Mode and choose to make one floorplan. Change to Select Mode and place the pins, lines & add arrowheads by using the Manipulate Palette, row 2, 6th palette from the left.

B. In Floor Plan Mode option drag the floorplan to make a copy. Select copy endpoints from the floorplan menu. Then delete old pins. Change the lower pin to a male pin using the Manipulate Palette (top row, last palette).

C. Change facing of the male dancer by selecting pin and using the Manipulate Palette (top row, 3rd from the left) to turn it.

Dance notation software

▌ Drama software

WEBSITE

MediaStage is a program produced by Immersive Education (www.immersiveeducation.com) that allows you to create a 3D film set. You can select your choice of scenery, lighting, props and characters. Then program in your own storyline before recording the spoken voices of the characters reading out your script. Set camera angles and view the play from those perspectives.

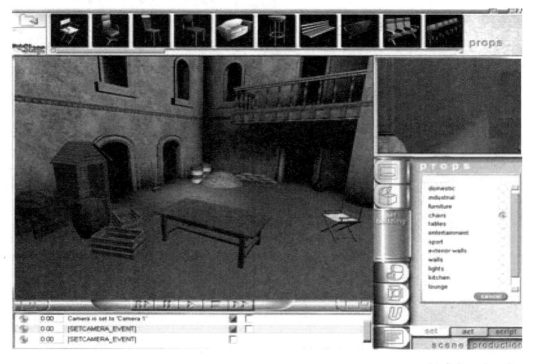

MediaStage in action

MediaStage is a powerful tool that has many applications for drama, music composition or PSHE. Learners can trial ideas and see how they could be staged. You could set up a scene before asking actors to complete the story as an improvisation. Actors can rehearse their voiceover skills. A scene can be created and a musician asked to compose background music for it.

Composition, performance and evaluation

Composition

Whether in music, drama or dance, all compositions need a starting point, stimulus or idea. ICT can generate this in a number of ways. It could be a photo, a short piece of film, a silhouette using light and screens, a digitally created sound effect or musical extract, the start of an animated story created by media software, the start of a story spoken and recorded on audio, or a picture or movie projected onto a screen. Improvisation is an important performing technique and a form of composition.

Improvisation also needs a stimulus, which you can introduce while the performance is taking place. ICT can generate random stimuli for the actor, dancer or musician to react to, such as short, musical, computer-generated motifs introduced randomly, or a videoconference link to another musician to take part in a question-and-answer session. Sensors can be used which – when triggered by movement – play music, random sounds or generate photos or video. The dancer reacts to these stimuli and improvises to what they see or hear. In drama, a photo, video or commentary can be produced, which the actor has to react to or continue to develop to a successful conclusion.

The development process

Once performers have their stimuli, they should work through possible ideas which they then organize and structure. Video can be used to capture this process but performers can also use ICT as a tool. Musicians can make audio recordings of musical motifs or play them 'real time' on a computer into a notation or sequencing program before developing the ideas and playing them back to review progress. Actors can photograph stage sets and check over the composition of the scene. Scriptwriters can use a PDA, Tablet PC or PC to type out their scripts, or they could dictate their ideas to an audio recorder or trial them in a 3D media program. Dancers can set up a video camera to film their dance steps before playing them back to review the sequences.

Reworking and refining

After the piece has been constructed and rehearsed, video evidence, music software and 3D media allows the composer, performer, writer, actor, choreographer or dancer to review the piece and make refinements. Rehearsals can continue to be recorded and small refinements made right up to the performance.

Performance

The performance can contain ICT to enhance it or to be an integral part. Project videos or photos for scenery; include computer-generated pictures, music and sound sensors; set up a videoconference link to another venue to connect performers or to widen the audience. The performance can also be recorded for review, analysis, feedback and as a record or celebration of achievement.

Evaluation

Reviewing how the piece developed, how could it have been improved and how the performance went can all be done by replaying the video, sound recording and data on the ICT equipment. The process can be colleted and stored using ICT for future reference and as feedback for the performers.

Top tips

Interesting ideas to experiment with

➡ ICT – whether generating music, sound, pictures, film or lighting effects – can create a mood or setting.

➡ Use movement sensors set out on stage linked to sounds, music, photos or videos. As the performer moves around the stage, they trigger the movement sensors to play whatever has been programmed so that the performer works with the stimulus or reacts to it. OptiMusic works on this principle – sound or music is played when the light beam is broken. This can be atmospheric if you have a smoke machine, so that the light beam shines brighter through the smoke.

➡ Use mobile devices such as PDAs, iPods or Tablet PCs to help plan, construct or storyboard the piece.

➡ Include a back-projected video or collage of photos that form part of the performance.

▌Videoconferencing

Videoconferencing can be used to show, collaborate or improvise compositions. Here are some suggestions:

➡ Set up a videoconference link to another group of performers to play in ensemble or improvise with. This could be groups of dancers in one venue and musicians in another. Actors could be placed in different locations but linked by videoconferencing – perhaps the stage is set for one scene and another scene is set on location or in another country.

➡ Set up videoconference workshops or master classes between teachers or professional and pupils. Alternatively, link learners by videoconference and let them show their work to other students.

➡ Set up videoconference facilities for moderating exam work or performances, with examiners or moderators at a central location and students performing at their local school or exam centre.

Top tips

Adding magic!

➡ Although this chapter is about using ICT to enhance the performance of learners in creative situations, it can also be handy to add a little bit of performance magic to help with demonstrations, starters and plenaries.

➡ Countdowns: there are many situations where a simple countdown on television or screen can add a note of anticipation or urgency to the lesson. Making a countdown is simple:

   ➡ Use PowerPoint to make a simple slide show with big numbers. Set the show to play back at the desired speed (making numbers run slower or faster than expected can lead to tension or urgency).

   ➡ Use movie-editing software to create short sequences with a number on-screen. Add transitions to fade or wipe across as the count progresses – try adding suitable music too.

➡ Torches: very bright torches are relatively cheap to buy and are a powerful, handheld spotlight to draw your learners' attention to a specific object or activity.

➡ UV lights and smoke machines can also be used to incredible effect during presentations.

- Image slide shows can make excellent backdrops for performances. These can be achieved without the need for a laptop by using either an iPod or a memory card reader attached to a data projector.

- Use the video capability of a mobile phone to instantly revisit rehearsed moments.

- MP3 recorders, mobile phones and PDAs can be used to record sound effects and narration.

Chapter 7

Unravel to create

This chapter includes activities that pull a subject or concept apart, allowing pupils to move through and reassemble it in a guided, non-linear manner. This is done in a way that allows them to use their own learning style to good effect – not only for their benefit but for the whole group. We all digest information and solve problems differently and these activities encourage us to use this as a strength.

By 'guided, non-linear', we mean providing the freedom for learners to find their own way through the learning experience while making sure there is a well-defined framework in place that avoids the most common pitfalls associated with non-linear learning, such as straying so far from the original target subject that no learning (at least for that subject) takes place.

The following activities are taken from three different sectors of education and, although the degree of non-linear activity varies in each activity, the basic concept of dismantling and reassembling creatively prevails.

Robo dancing

Robo dancing

This activity was developed to help introduce the concept of control technology and robots to Year 1 pupils. It used the following ICT resources, which don't require access to computers:

➡ a Robosapien robot (we used three together for better visual impact);

➡ some images of robots and other programmable equipment such as a washing machine to form a photographic slide show – we used an iPod, but an inexpensive media card reader would work just as well;

➡ a data projector;

➡ a whiteboard.

Alternatively, you could use a laptop or desktop computer, an interactive whiteboard or a Tablet PC to show the slide show.

The session started with the class being divided into groups and given the task of deciding what a robot is and what it does. Their descriptions were displayed on an interactive whiteboard or flip chart for later reference.

Deciding what a robot is and what it does

A slide show was shown of a range of robots and other machines, following which the class was again divided into groups and asked to decide from the pictures what makes these machines similar. The results were displayed on the board.

A discussion took place based on the two sets of notes on the board in which pupils defined what is a robot. The aim was to conclude that a robot is a machine that follows a list of instructions. We then explained the concept that the list of instructions is known as a program and that robots need a program to work.

We then introduced the Robosapiens by providing a demonstration of their pre-programmed dance routine. We explained that this is the only dance that the Robosapiens know and that the group challenge for today is to help the robots to learn another dance.

The dance routine

The class was again divided into groups to look at how Robosapiens move compared with humans. This was done by physically comparing similar movements like steps and arm movements and allowing the groups to decide how this affects dance movements. This information was gathered together and shared.

Ideas were worked through to show possible movements Robosapiens could make, which were joined together to form a short dance routine. The routine was practised until the whole group had learned it.

Working through the dance movements

The class was divided into groups and allowed to experiment with the Robosapiens to work out how to simulate the dance moves. Each group was shown how to turn these moves into a simple program and to send it to a robot. The groups were then allowed to experiment by programming the robot and modifying their routines if they needed to, as long as they also worked through each new move as a group. They were then ready for the final programmed routine to be trialled on one of the robots. Finally, the pupils and Robosapiens did the dance routine together.

Programming the robots

Dancing together

Tools

- Programmable toys.
- Mind mapping software, such as Inspiration.
- Webcam or camcorder.
- Data projector.

KEY Points

- For all activities, find the big picture then break it into chunks.
- Group dynamics and opportunities for teamwork are key.

Top tips

Unravelling to create

➡ List the theories or concepts you want learners to understand – an integral part of the activity.

➡ It doesn't matter where or how learners uncover a theory or concept during the activity – the important thing is that they do and that they work with it.

➡ When providing information resources, variety is key.

➡ Support learners' research skills. Help them to differentiate between genuine and weak material.

➡ Failure is success that has not quite happened yet. Help learners to understand that reflection is the most important development tool.

➡ Well-supported, solid communication between all participants is vital. Use every available method.

➡ Make your role that of facilitator.

Further activities

Time detectives

This activity is based around a history lesson, but it could just as easily be used for teaching science, engineering, technology or geography. It's aimed at secondary-level teaching but it could be adapted, scaled down or scaled up.

The resources used could include the following in addition to paper-based materials: e-books; physical artefacts; costumes (to enable role play); drawings, paintings and photographs; websites; a virtual museum tour; a videoconference link to a museum or 'expert witness'.

The theme is set by introducing an event from history as a mystery that needs to be solved within a given timescale. We used the Battle of Hastings.

The class is divided into two teams of detectives and each team is provided with details of their objective. These should differ slightly between teams to provide opportunities for information to be unearthed from different angles:

➡ Team 1: what happened at the Battle of Hastings? How did William snatch victory from the jaws of defeat?

➡ Team 2: what happened at the Battle of Hastings? Why did Harold's clever defence strategy fail?

Each team is provided with staged clues, questions, tasks, tools and resources they can access, together with a research guide (a teacher or teaching assistant) to help them to find appropriate resources. The clues or tasks lead learners to a choice of information and resources, and by uncovering each layer the next clue or question is found.

The clues are often tasks in themselves and, because each task is different, they allow various learners in the team to use their own learning styles to good effect. Examples include:

➡ The landscape is often important to successful defence in battle. Find out where Harold chose to place his troops to defend against William's army. List the advantages and disadvantages of his position.

➡ Did the Saxons and Normans use different battle formations and strategies? Find out what they were and, using the model soldiers and landscape provided, try them out.

➡ What weaponry did each side use? Create some examples and discuss their strengths and weaknesses.

➡ How was each army made up? Were they professionally paid soldiers or conscripts? Use role play to reveal how you would feel as a soldier in each army.

With each clue or task, the research guide suggests possible sources for answers. Each extract of information is pieced together using a flow diagram or mind map – the role of the research guide here is to help learners to develop their own way of doing this.

Teams are not allowed to share evidence they collect, but they may catalogue and negotiate to swap one or two pieces of evidence during the challenge.

At the end of the activity, each team is asked to present its findings to the other, with each team nominating a specialist to present each layer of evidence. Ensure all members of the team are involved in the presentation and that they use a method they are comfortable with.

Finally, you can draw the two sets of findings together to form an overarching story of the subject. The activity is reinforced using the evidence and presentations to form a storyboard showing how the activity took place, the evidence gathered and so on. The storyboard can become a physical part of the classroom environment (a notice board), an electronic record (a screen with slide show or web page) or both.

WEBSITE

For another angle on a similar idea, have a look at the interactive Time detectives web game on the Channel 4 Time Team website at www.channel4.com/history/timeteam.

▌ Design challenge

This project is aimed at technology students, but it could be adapted to suit other groups of learners by reducing or increasing the degree of difficulty.

The idea is to solve a practical problem by designing, manufacturing and testing an engineering product. The twist is that part of the challenge involves working remotely with other team members. The use of videoconferencing links enables the team members to interact and communicate throughout the project.

Many schools rely on sharing CAD/CAM facilities with other schools, colleges or support services. Unfortunately, sharing facilities can present problems. Timing is such that viewing the manufacture of your design isn't possible, which is a loss for the learner of the vital link between design and making. Videoconferencing allows this link to be firmly retained.

Setting up a design and construction team using specialists in different locations, all communicating via the latest technology, reflects a scenario that exists in many industries, and this aspect injects a sense of realism into the challenge. It also provides an opportunity for inter-school, school–college or education–industry partnerships to work more effectively, better utilizing technology resources between partners.

In this challenge, there is maximum use of remote access. The brief is as follows:

Design and build a bridge capable of carrying the Mars explorer vehicle and its load over a Martian crater. Due to the chemical composition of the planet's atmosphere, only a special polymer alloy may be used to manufacture the bridge's components.

The manufacturing equipment is located at a secret facility accessible via video link. Use CAD to generate your design and then, using the videoconferencing link, liaise with the technicians at the secret facility to ensure that the bridge components are manufactured to your specification.

Once your components have been manufactured, arrangements will be made to transport your team to a test facility. There you will be able to assemble scale versions of the component parts and carry out tests using the Mars simulator robots. During the tests you will be competing against rival teams to find which design is the most effective.

Liaising via a videoconferencing link

The general idea is that the design process takes place at school or college, supported remotely from the centre that manufactures the designed components.

Each team is provided with the following resources:

➡ A sample of the material to be used.

➡ A detailed set of parameters that will affect their design, such as the distance the bridge has to span, the weight it needs to carry, dimensions of the Mars explorer vehicle and maps of the Martian crater.

➡ A range of background materials and resources relating to engineering fundamentals, such as websites, online journals, magazines, textbooks, newspaper articles and interactive engineering software.

➡ Examples of similar structures that have been constructed, both successfully and unsuccessfully.

➡ Access to compatible CAD software.

➡ Videoconferencing facilities.

➡ Videoconferencing, email and instant messaging access to the technical staff responsible for manufacturing the bridge.

➡ A named facilitator to guide the team towards suitable resources at each stage of the challenge.

Videoconferencing software systems mean you can hold a discussion while viewing the person at the other end, but many systems also allow you to use the following features:

➡ text messaging;

➡ sending and receiving files;

➡ sharing an on-screen whiteboard (ideal for brainstorming);

➡ multiple cameras (in this case, one or two cameras can be directed at the machine while another is directed towards the supporting technician).

Pupils at work

A pair of 3G phones used in video call mode makes an excellent back-up plan in case the videoconferencing link fails.

A breakdown of the stages in the challenge is given below:

➤ Overall concept: teams are briefed on the challenge and provided with the resources required. The brief is carried out via a videoconferencing link to base.

➤ Team formation: each team is allocated its support personnel (teacher/ facilitator) and manufacturing technician, along with details on how to access them during the project.

➤ Research: teams unravel the background information that may influence their design.

➤ Storming: one or two ideas for potential designs are generated, and sketches and outline drawings are created and compared to past designs. These are subjected to scrutiny by the team with the help of the facilitator.

➤ Design: ideas are developed into real designs using CAD. At each stage the design is passed to and discussed with the facilitator.

➤ Design briefing with manufacturing facility: initial designs are sent to the manufacturing technician and potential design problems are discussed with the technician via videoconference.

➤ Final design: following discussions with the manufacturing technician, the team selects a final design and carries out any modifications prior to the manufacture of its components.

➤ Prototype component manufacture using remote videoconference: each team produces one set of components and observes the process via a videoconference link.

➤ Videoconference meeting with the manufacturing facility: teams discuss any problems with the initial set of components and agree on any necessary modifications.

➤ Final prototype component manufacture using remote videoconference: each team produces its final set of components and observes the process via a videoconference link.

➤ Prototype test day: teams are brought together at one location for a day of testing. Each team spends the morning assembling its components to form the finished design. In the afternoon, the bridge designs are placed across the crater and the Mars explorer vehicle is manoeuvred fully laden across the bridge to test its integrity.

▎ **Remote desktop tool**

Plagiarism often gets a bad press, but seeing others at work can kick-start creativity. ICT offers a number of tools to let learners spot good ideas in each other's work in a managed way.

If you have access to a network and some form of displaying images on a large screen, it's not hard to share some of your pupils' work with the rest of the class in a positive way. This doesn't mean stopping everyone to look, and it doesn't mean showing only the product when the process is the thing.

The software you need is called a remote desktop tool. When you use this program on your screen, you will see a window containing a number of small screen thumbnails. Click on one of these and you can watch what the user is seeing on-screen – you can even take over their mouse and keyboard if required.

WEBSITE

Ask your ICT technician for assistance with this facility and don't expect it to be set up in a few minutes. Try Google to search for suitable free software (www.google.co.uk) using the search string 'free remote desktop software'.

A remote desktop tool

Plug your computer into a projector and go through the thumbnails to find interesting examples to display to the class. You could take over their computers but it is better to allow learners to demonstrate themselves without having to stand at the front of the class.

Alternatively, disable the ability to take over another computer and let any learner see what is happening on someone else's screen whenever they want. The ability to watch someone doing something, without disturbance or interruption, is pretty cool.

Unravelling your marking

How many pupils complete work, good or bad, in lesson time? How many learn from the comments you make when you mark their work? Do teachers get to see only the finished product or can we see the steps taken to get there? Much good learning material is lost but you and your learners are generating it constantly.

One example of this was in an art lesson that didn't use much ICT. The teacher photographed and printed a small copy of everyone's work every lesson and left it in a place where everyone could see it. All the work was there, stage by stage – comments, ideas for improvement, final projects – and learners were able to browse this during lessons.

Set up a password-protected web page that everyone can upload their work to each lesson, with space for you to add comments, and make it as accessible as you feel comfortable with. This enables pupils to look at and evaluate what's there.

Unravelling write-ups

Producing a report on something comes up time and again in the classroom – although surprisingly the way teachers ask learners to do it varies widely according to the subject being studied and the teacher. Whatever form of write-up is required, ICT can help with the creative part of the process.

On a simple level, this can be something as straightforward as asking learners to document the action as it happens with the technology available, such as the school's digital camera or their mobile phone. If anyone has an MP3 player that can record sound (many phones can too), a real-time commentary is easy to produce. Learners then have these resources to assist them in producing their write-up – even if the poor-quality images never make it into the finished piece, this is about better writing and understanding not decorative work. These recordings can then be discussed and evaluated more deeply.

If there is a long period between the event happening and the write-up (say, more than 15 minutes), mixing the order of the photos and adding a few of your own can make the level of thinking and response better. The correct order in which events happened might seem obvious to you, but the simple act of putting them in the right order quickly gets everyone back up to speed.

A slide show of images can be left running while learners work to produce a write-up. The images can be used as part of a simple sequencing activity, a fun 'spot the fake photo' game or a 'spot the mistake' task. Similarly, playing back a commentary recorded at the time can help learners to take themselves back to when the events happened.

Top tips

Things to avoid

➡ Don't let pupils lose their way – keep them focused on the task.

➡ Misunderstandings result from poor communication. Be clear, concise and available!

➡ Ensure there is a balance of learning styles in the group dynamic.

➡ Maximum intervention equals minimum creativity.

➡ No intervention equals chaos.

from the web.

● Encourage information sharing via SMS text, Bluetooth or multimedia messaging.

● Use mobile phones to capture visual and audio evidence.

● During activities like time detectives, 3G phones can provide a cost-effective alternative to videoconferencing if a broadband connection is not available.

● Use image slide shows from a card reader or iPod to reinforce steps in the activity.

Chapter 8

From your pocket to the wall

Mobile phones and MP3 players are often banned from the classroom environment and in many cases from the entire school. Colleges are much more of a mixed bag, with the norm being a unilateral understanding that phones and other devices will remain switched off during lessons.

So why would anyone in their right minds attempt to provide ideas on their use in teaching and learning? Often the potential of a mobile device is only partially utilized by its owner. How many of us own a mobile phone with stills or video camera capability but use it only to text and phone? Or own an MP3 player and only listen to music? The potential to tap into an ICT resource that frees you from the constraints of computer-suite access or laptop fatigue has got to be a good thing.

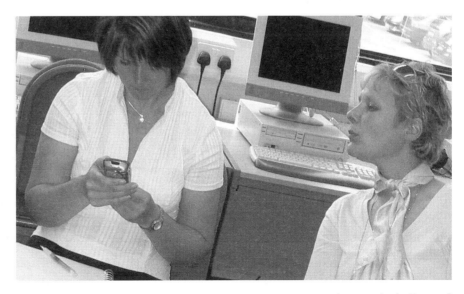

Are you a 'gadget' person?

Many of these devices are low cost for high gain, often doing the same job as a PC or laptop, creating the flexibility to work anywhere and freeing up the rest of your ICT kit for other learners. So maybe its time to 'unban' the gadgets!

Learners today are confident in using these devices and it is this confidence that makes adapting and adopting them as learning tools important. Pupils are growing up with them as the norm and that in itself is reason to sit up and take notice.

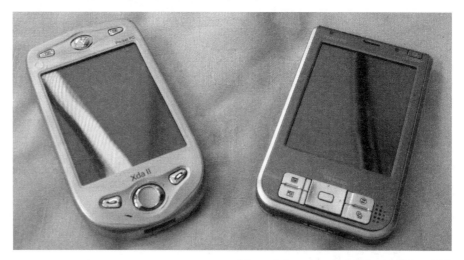

A 'smart' phone – a combination of PDA and 3G

Some examples of positive uses for these fast-growing technologies include sharing work, creating short films, taking and sharing photos, sound recording, report writing, homework, viewing films, listening to language lessons, collecting evidence for a portfolio, study support, reading/listening to e-books and carrying out a presentation.

Mobile Learning Project

The Mobile Learning Project was set up by the Learning Discovery Centre. It began with two Year 5 classes from different primary schools being issued with PDAs or handheld computers.

Sharing learning is fun!

The idea behind the project, which took place over a school year, was to improve ICT confidence within the groups, enhance student collaboration, increase the integration of ICT into other subject areas, and encourage extended and independent learning. It was also an opportunity to study pupils' acceptance of new technologies and to learn from how they developed their own ways of using the devices. Right from the start, students and teachers were encouraged to use the PDAs in any class or individual learning activity they felt was appropriate.

Each PDA was equipped with the full complement of pocket PC software and, over a controlled period, learners were introduced to new features (we were also introduced to some by the students!). They were allowed to control simple maintenance tasks such as charging and to take them home for homework. They were also provided with network and internet access.

Over the period of the project, only a few devices were lost or damaged. Indeed, pupils took great pride in looking after their own equipment and supporting each other.

- You need at least one method of getting images and audio from your device to your audience.

- You also need at least one way to catch audio, images and video.

- Plenty of examples of both of these are in this chapter.

- Handheld devices are not inferior computers – they are just different. If you expect to use them in activities as direct substitutes, you will be disappointed. Plan activities to the strengths of the equipment you have.

- Take the time to practise transferring material between devices as this is often the point where difficulties occur.

Further activities

ICT Lite

ICT Lite was another Learning Discovery Centre project based around the idea of carrying out lessons without a PC or laptop (although a projector in the room was allowed) using only devices that were small enough to be carried in a bag!

With many mobile phones equipped with stills or video cameras, voice recorders, MP3 players, note-taking functions, media card storage and wireless technologies, it seemed a pity that these are often overlooked as teaching and learning tools. Used together with the range of highly portable music and video players, PDAs, television/projector-playable media card readers, wireless technologies, and portable and rechargeable high-quality photo printers – and the scene was set!

Much of our work in this strand has been event-based, working with groups of teachers and learners of all ages on short, focused, challenge activities and presentations, and the collection of work evidence for e-portfolios, individual learning plans, and formative and summative assessment.

The equipment we used included:

➡ PDAs: small, handheld computers with similar functionality to larger computers. The most popular PDAs use Microsoft Pocket PC software, which is a cut-down version of Windows. What PDAs gain in pocket portability and flexibility they lose in screen size and memory power, although memory can usually be added using a media storage card. Many PDAs have a range of accessories available, such as VGA links for presentations using a projector, wireless cards, SIM card units (converting them to phones) and cameras.

➡ Mobile phones: most phones now have a stills camera, and many have both video and stills capability and voice recording. Some even have MP3 players. For our project work, we chose to use 3G phones with video-calling capability. In classroom work, we deactivated the SIM cards to avoid the temptation to text and call. The phones had a combination of Bluetooth and memory storage card capability, together with the ability to send and receive MMS messages (when the SIM card was fitted).

➡ Printers: we are not talking about the traditional desk-based USB connection printer here, but lightweight photo printers with a built-in memory card reader, LCD image viewer and Bluetooth adapter to avoid the need for a PC or laptop. We also opted for rechargeable battery packs to ensure maximum portability.

➡ iPod: the iPod is the original digital music player and the model we used is a combination music player, voice recorder and photo viewer. It can be connected to a television or projector via a cradle and lead and, when using a combination of photo slides and sound, can create excellent PC-free presentations. We also bought the optional photo-link unit, which allows you to download photos from camera to iPod without a PC or Mac.

➡ MP3: these are music players and voice recorders. The device we used was a basic, low-cost 128MB unit that also acted as a USB memory key, enabling fast movement of recordings from device to laptop or PC when required or replayed through powered speakers.

➡ Digital media card player: these low-cost devices plug into a television or projector and read directly from the media cards used in cameras and phones to create PC-free slide shows.

Our ICT Lite kit

Top tips

From pocket to wall

➡ Keep it simple – less is more, so try not to do too much at once.

➡ Listen to your learners. What do they like using and why? Things that work for you may not work for them.

➡ Make sharing equipment, material or processes positive by the way you set up the activity.

➡ Remove any reasons to fear the technology.

➡ Use learners' own devices. Encourage learning ownership.

➡ Make the work 'sticky' by making sure the activity is about some mental processing and not about learning how to use the gadget.

➡ Borrow a device and give it a try before you buy.

➡ Have a back-up plan.

▌Share and share alike

Sharing using PDAs

Sharing is a major tool in spreading the 'learning bug'. Any portable device equipped with an infrared port or Bluetooth technology has the ability to enable learners to share files.

Both infrared and Bluetooth are used extensively by business and commerce as a way of moving information such as documents, address cards, photos, film clips, spreadsheets, charts, graphs, notes and appointments from a portable device to a computer. Many learners are already familiar with the technology for sharing ring tones or pictures and readily adapt to its use in the classroom.

Media storage cards also offer opportunities to share between mobile devices or from mobile device to computer. Using a media card player connected to a television or projector means you can create adhoc slide shows. Most photo printers have card reading facilities built in, allowing you to print photos instantly for sharing and sometimes to edit the photo first.

Either way, in our classroom, sharing translates to a great way of developing group activities.

Story chase

For this activity, each pupil adds their own work to a collective piece until everyone has added something. The completed work is then shared with the whole group using Bluetooth or infrared technology.

Here are a couple of variations on the theme:

➡ Follow the leader: you write the first paragraph to set the scene and pass it to the first pupil, who then adds a paragraph and passes it to the next student and so on.

➡ Picture this: you write a theme for the story and, using Bluetooth or infrared, beam a picture to each pupil as a stimulus. Each learner then writes their piece and these are beamed back to you to collate into a whole story.

Paper-free homework

For this activity, you beam the homework tasks to learners, who then beam the completed homework back to you when they have completed it.

Another variation on this theme is to use the mobile device as a homework diary. You could beam this week's diary entries to the class or, if the devices can access the school/college network, to the class calendar in Microsoft Outlook.

Language learning

The recording capabilities of PDAs and mobile phones make them a perfect medium for adhoc voice recording. Learners in our Mobile Learning Project devised this method of keeping language skills up to scratch between lessons. The teacher (or a learner) records a phrase or series of phrases and then shares them with the rest of the group using infrared technology. These phrases can then be practised by pupils whenever they like.

Language learning with mobility

▌ Storyboarding

During a class activity such as a science experiment, learners are encouraged to photograph what is happening in sequence using camera phones equipped with Bluetooth or media storage cards.

The photos can then be beamed using Bluetooth directly to a Bluetooth-enabled photo printer or printed using a card-reading photo printer. The photos can be displayed on a storyboard, enabling learners to relive the experiment. Alternatively, the photos could be shared on a television or projector using a media card player – some projectors and televisions have these built in.

▌ The evidence is clear!

Instant evidence!

Collecting evidence for formative or summative assessment can be difficult and time consuming. This can be compounded if learners have activities divided between different locations. Students aged between 14 and 19 are probably most prone to this because their learning is often divided between school, college and work placement.

Collecting evidence using mobile devices results in material that can be shared easily and viewed straight away for formative feedback.

➡ Beam it: learners collect evidence (photos, video clips, text reports, audio interviews and so on) using either a mobile phone or a PDA. This is then passed to their assessor via Bluetooth or infrared. The evidence can be returned in the same way to learners after it has been marked.

➡ MMS it: learners send the assessor an MMS message containing evidence, which the assessor collects from an MMS mobile phone or via the phone company's MMS web portal. The message can be sent to several recipients such as school and college.

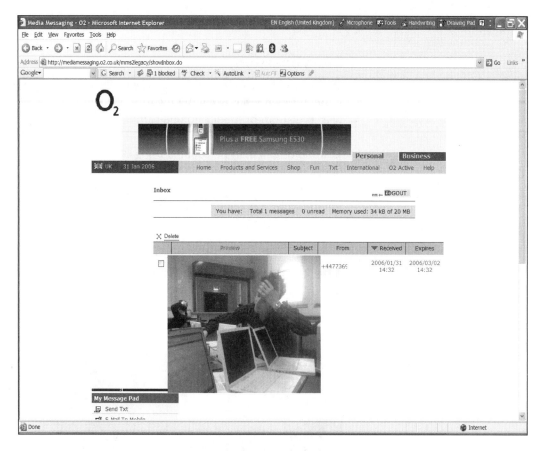

The evidence from a learner, ready to collect and assess

➡ GPRS email: using a GPRS-enabled phone, learners email the evidence to the assessor(s) or upload it to their personal web page.

➡ MP3 record it: learners record feedback from work supervisors or witnesses using MP3 players/recorders and allow the assessor to download these onto a PC or laptop. This isn't as broad, fast or slick as the other methods, but nevertheless a cost-effective method where audio evidence is appropriate.

Web radio reports

WEBSITE

Internet radio services such as Radio Waves (www.radiowaves.co.uk) have increased in popularity and allow learners to be creative with sound in a unique way. Recording sound clips for web radio can be carried out using the recording function of a PDA, the sound recorder on some mobile phones or an MP3 player/recorder. Examples of applications include the following.

Audio books

The class is divided into groups. Each group is given a list of the components of a story, which could be a couple of paragraphs to a complete chapter, depending on ability. Each group is allocated a part of the story to create and tell. The groups then plan out and write the elements of their part. When they are ready to act them out, they use MP3 recorders to record each contribution. A fun element can be introduced by using dialects to match the characters and adding their own sound effects. The recorded contributions can be joined together using free sound-editing software such as Audacity

WEBSITE

(www.audacity.sourceforge.net) to make an audio book.

Recording stories

Time reporters 1

Ask pupils to imagine being sent back in time to interview a famous person from history. What would they say? How would life be different? This is an excellent role-play activity where the class is divided into groups and allocated two tasks:

➡ to act as time-travelling reporters who have to interview a famous person from history;

➡ to research and role-play a historical character for the other groups to interview.

The key to the success of this activity is in facilitating research for both the interview questions and the role play. The interviews are recorded using the recording facility on a PDA or MP3 player/recorder.

Time reporters 2

This time the theme is post-war Britain. Ask learners to create a multimedia newspaper for the school, collecting photos, films and radio clips, and interviewing relatives and friends who experienced this era.

➡ The class is divided into groups, with each group selecting a subject on which to concentrate. Examples include sport, clothing, home life, work, school, toys and games, and food. Using wireless-enabled PDAs, learners access news archive photographs and film footage that have been downloaded previously and placed in network folders.

➡ Using the archive materials as research, the groups develop questions about their chosen subject and share these using infrared between PDAs. The recording facility of the PDA is used to record the interviews, which again can be shared via infrared with those unable to find a relative or friend able to recall life during the period.

➡ The material is downloaded from the PDAs to the network and inserted into a multimedia newspaper template.

➡ The interview activity would also work using the recording facility on a mobile phone or MP3 recorder/player.

Podcasting

Podcasting means uploading music, stories or articles for download onto a mobile device to be listened to later. This is a great way to share audio material with learners. It is also used in many universities to provide audio lectures for students who are unable to attend.

Podcasting sites were originally dedicated almost exclusively to iPod users, but now most provide podcasts as MP3 files, allowing them to be downloaded to any device that plays or converts MP3 files. This has extended podcasting to MP3 players, PDAs and many mobile phones.

Podcasting

▌iPod storage

Imagine you have spent a few hours with your learners producing some excellent movies about living in the 1940s. You now have several laptops with edited movies on board and need to move these quickly onto one computer so that you can show them during the next session. The problem is, your laptop doesn't have a DVD burner (and if it did, it would take too long to burn the movies).

One way of collecting the movies in one place is to use a portable hard drive, but this means buying, storing and carrying around another device – so is there another way?

We have a useful alternative in the shape of the iPod. This can play music, pictures and videos, but it can also act as a portable, high-speed hard drive. Movies play directly from iPod storage as quickly as if they were located on the hard drive of your computer.

The amount of storage varies depending on the size of iPod you have and the amount of media you carry on it (this will have an effect on available space). To determine how much space is being used on your iPod, connect it to your PC or Mac and open iTunes. All the information you need will displayed on the bottom of the main iTunes window.

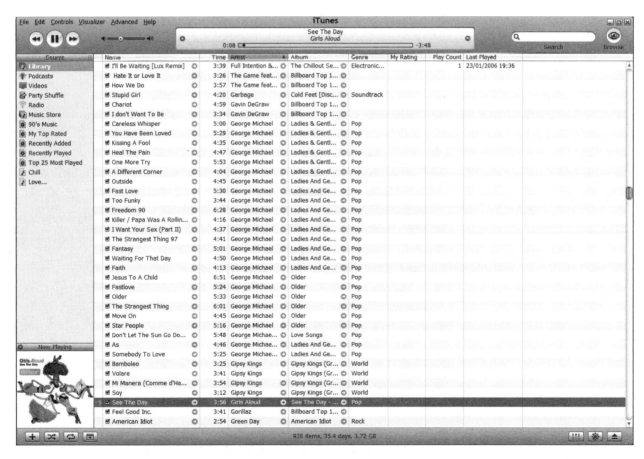

The iTunes menu

Using spare capacity will reduce the space available for adding more music to your iPod, so it's worth setting yourself two simple rules of thumb before going any further:

➡ if any files and/or folders are to be permanent, set yourself a limit on the space you allow them to take up;

➡ get into the habit of clearing out files stored temporarily.

The next step is to tell the iPod that you want to use it for storage. To do this:

➡ select the iPod on the source list located on the left-hand side of the iTunes window;

➡ click on the iPod icon at the bottom of the iTunes window – this opens up a separate window called iPod;

➡ under the heading Music, tick the box titled Enable disk use;

➡ click OK.

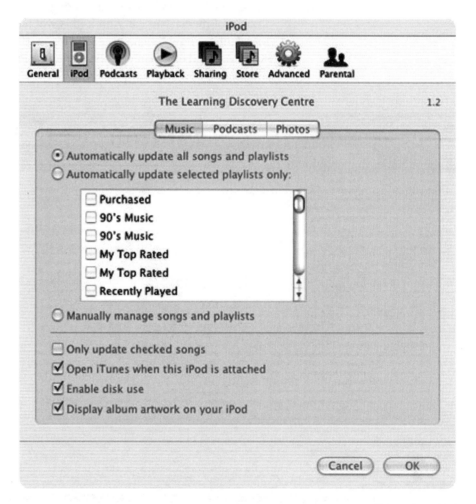

Disk use is enabled

The iPod appears in Windows Explorer or on a Mac desktop as a separate drive.

You can save to, move or copy and paste files straight to the iPod storage drive.

Top tips

Things to avoid

➡ You spend the lesson trying to get a gadget to work. Go to plan B and get your learners to try it. Next time, try it before the lesson!

➡ Powerless devices – don't forget to charge them up and have spare batteries.

➡ No signal – check the mobile signal in the room you will be using.

➡ Loads of material at the end, none of it relevant to the subject. Have tight objectives that help learners to focus.

➡ 'Bluejacking' – make sure the devices are paired to avoid unwanted Bluetooth connections from outside.

➡ Arguments over whose turn it is to use the device next. Make rotation part of the plan or let learners use their own devices.

➡ Lock the phone to numbers you want to use to stop learners video messaging their favourite aunt or uncle in Argentina!

Computer-free presentations

Presenting without the aid of a laptop and PowerPoint is rare. The advent of such useful technology cannot be dismissed, but carrying around a laptop, projector, notes and a register can be inconvenient and a great way to keep chiropractors in business!

We were encouraged to look at using mobile technologies as a presentation tool from two angles:

➡ There is the 'Let's present without getting a hernia' motivation – using smaller devices is no doubt more spinal friendly.

➡ There is the learning challenge, which is about the creative use of a resource which, although popular with learners, is underutilized in a learning sense.

The learning challenge is about creating a presentation using nothing but mobile devices. For this we usually provide our group with a couple of 3G camera phones (one Bluetooth and one with a media card), a pair of rechargeable photo printers, a storage card reader, a projector, an iPod or MP3 recorder/player and any equipment learners have to hand such as their own mobile phones.

A theme is provided for the challenge – we have used titles such as 'Using your brain' but you could go with almost anything. A timescale is set for familiarization with the equipment and creation of the presentation itself. Some simple rules are set:

➡ Only the equipment provided and any in your pockets may be used.

➡ Every member of your team must participate in the presentation.

Ideas for the resulting presentations vary from visual photographs and slide shows to sound recordings, rhymes and song writing.

The important lesson learned from this activity is that presenting isn't just about how many differing effects you can get from PowerPoint or how many tiny words you can squeeze on each page. It's about engagement, involvement and learning. There is a place for PowerPoint but its overuse may be a common disengagement problem that should be avoided.

Primary folk get creative

iPods and PDAs

One way of presenting without all the heavy equipment can be by using either an iPod or a PDA with a VGA adapter. Imagine walking into your classroom, removing a portable device from your pocket, attaching it to your projector and beginning the lesson!

In the case of the iPod, a simple slide show can be achieved using an adapter and a USB lead straight from your camera. This has the disadvantage of not allowing you to change the order of the slides or add sound or transition effects, but nevertheless it's still a useful method. Some cameras have onboard editing, allowing unwanted snaps to be deleted, images to be rotated and the order of photos in an album to be moved, making instant presentations straight from an iPod even more useful.

From camera to iPod in seconds

You can produce a professional presentation by setting up an album in Windows or Apple iPhoto and uploading from your PC or Mac, together with voice recordings and soundtracks from iTunes. PowerPoint slides can be used on your iPod too by saving your slides as jpegs.

PowerPoint creates a folder with the title of your presentation containing an image of each of your slides and, by dragging that folder into iPhoto (on an Apple Mac) or Adobe Photoshop (on a PC), you can upload the entire folder as an album ready to be shown. The only drawback is that you will lose any animations and links, but there is nothing to stop you slotting in a few photos between the slide images in the folder. You can also add music or voiceovers using iTalk and iTunes.

Recording with an iPod...

...then presenting!

Clearview is a program that allows a PDA to show PowerPoint slide shows without transition effects or animations. No conversion work is required as the software does this for you. Just upload the slide show to the PDA using either its cradle/dock when connected to the computer or a wireless file transfer using Bluetooth. It's also possible with some PDAs equipped with a camera to set up a photo slide show for viewing via the projector. If a device allows you to view an image, saving your PowerPoint slides as images means you can view those too.

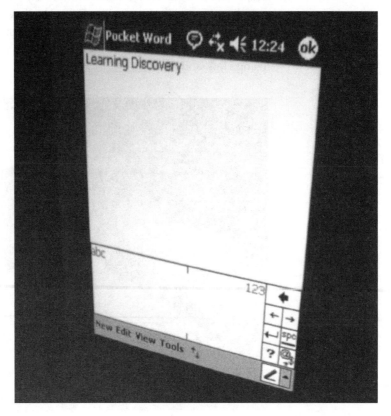

Simple solutions are best

Other presenting ideas

If you don't have access to an iPod or PDA, there are other ways of achieving similar results without resorting to a PC or laptop:

➡ Photo viewers: these are inexpensive and easy to use. They are memory card readers that plug into a television or projector using AV leads (the white, red and yellow sockets in the back of your television or projector). Some simply show the images as they are on the card, whereas others have a remote control that allows you to resize, zoom, rotate and shuffle the order. Some even play movie clips from cards.

➡ USB devices: if you have a projector capable of reading from USB devices, you can use:

➡ Memory card readers: any USB memory card reader that plugs into your PC or Mac will work here as long as it's compatible with your memory card. Make sure the images on the card are saved in the order you want them to display.

➡ Flash memory drives or USB-type MP3 players: the same rules apply. Make sure the images on the device are in the right order, plug the drive into the projector, set to slide show and away you

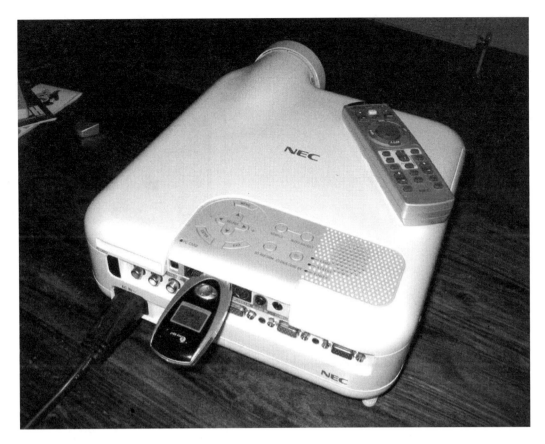

From MP3 player...

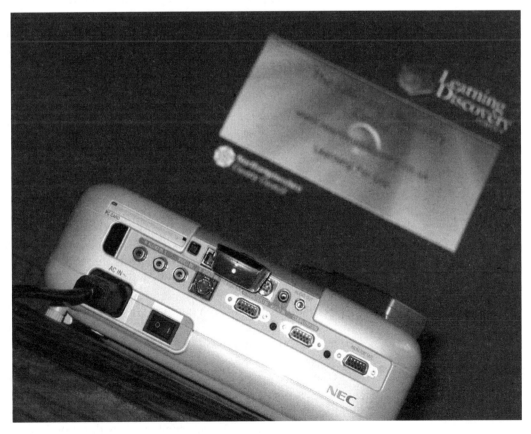

...to the wall!

Movie viewer

There used to be few options when wanting to play movie files during lessons, but thanks to the increasing use of mobile players these options are expanding.

iPod movie viewer

One example is the iPod range, which now has the ability to play movies. Connecting via an AV lead to a projector or television provides a lightweight and portable alternative to a laptop or desktop machine. The ability to collect movies from several sessions onto one iPod (using it as storage) and then to play them wherever convenient is a cost-effective alternative to tying up a computer that could be in use elsewhere.

Videoconferencing to go

Videoconferencing is a great way to interact with a class or location without actually being there, but it relies on having a broadband connection (wired or wireless) in both locations.

If the location you want to videoconference with doesn't have broadband, there is a mobile solution. 3G mobile phones allow live streaming of video and sound over what is effectively mobile broadband, giving much the same capability of basic videoconferencing but on a smaller scale.

3G phones are usually equipped with a video camera with two lenses: one facing the phone operator and one facing away. In some cases there is one lens that swivels to allow you to capture pictures.

Using a 3G phone to make a video call is simple, but you need to call someone who also has a 3G phone and a good signal. Dial the number in the same way that you would a conventional phone and, when they answer, you can see the person you are calling. By changing lens direction, you can show the person you are calling any object or activity you wish.

Using 3G videophones to videoconference where a broadband connection is unavailable has its limitations. The screen is small and really a singular experience, and there are also network coverage issues which, although improving all the time, have yet to reach full potential.

Despite these limitations, this idea has some good uses, including:

➡ supporting learners and giving live reports of practical work – learners can show you work in progress using a live video feed;

➡ composing video diaries using 3G video messaging – these can be accessed on the web.

Using video messaging to create a video diary

● Use your school network to set up an ICT Lite folder for new activities. Encourage your learners to upload material gathered during these activities into the folder for later use and sharing.

● Set up an MP3 or podcast folder on the school network and allow your students to access it via their chosen device. Homework tasks, revision notes or whole lessons can be recorded and stored in the folder for learners to download at their leisure.

Chapter 9

The creative early years classroom

It's important to provide ICT in real-life situations. Although it's not always possible to have a washing machine in the home corner, a cardboard replica allows learners to explore. Many toys replicate home appliances, including washing machines, fridges, microwaves and televisions. These provide pupils with invaluable experiences and allow them to start with what they know. Giving children experience with common ICT items, such as photocopiers, scanners and printers, allows them to explore what these items can do and, in the case of photocopiers, to produce some interesting results. One of the key elements of the Foundation Stage is maintaining the home–school link and involving parents with their children's education.

Maintaining the home–school link

One way to do this is to send the class mascot home with a digital camera so parents and learners can create a photographic diary. Another way is for learners to use digital cameras and sound recorders throughout the day as a diary. At the end of the day, this is projected so that parents can share the day with their children.

It is important to use whatever ICT you have available to add value to the experiences taking place. For example, digital sound recorders can be used to allow pupils to record and annotate their work in a way that is enjoyable for them and provides you with an accurate record of knowledge and understanding that can be used for various purposes.

What can often be overlooked is the children's adeptness with new technologies – the value of this is beyond measure and allows children in early years settings to interact in an ICT-rich environment with little time being spent on learning the technology.

Young children learn to interact in an ICT-rich environment

ICT Lite: early years version

Other exciting ICT opportunities that can be used with younger children include remote control robots and vehicles, mobile phones (working and obsolete), remote controls (working and obsolete) and PDAs. These allow learners to access technology in a way that is familiar to them. They will instantly pick up a mobile phone (real, fake, working or broken), dial a number and proceed to 'make' a telephone call. When pupil are given this opportunity in a more structured setting, the results can be amazing. For example, while reading the story of Little Red Riding Hood, you could stop at the key point where Little Red Riding Hood is about to knock on the door of Grandma's house. Pick up a mobile phone and hand it to a pupil, saying 'Let's phone Little Red Riding Hood!'. The pupil makes the call (what they actually dial is irrelevant, although number recognition can be reinforced at this point) and speaks to Little Red Riding Hood, talking about what they have learned from the story and advising Little Red Riding Hood on what to do. This use of ICT is real in a way that children recognize but imaginative in the way it is used. It allows learners to ask and answer questions, discuss situations and use their imaginations.

The different themes in a classroom (home corner, vet, doctor's surgery, school office and so on) can benefit from using a phone or similar technology. Digital cameras and camera phones are two items that are quick for pupils to learn and have a high enjoyment factor. Digital cameras can be used in a variety of settings (for example, capturing images of each other, capturing images based around a theme, explaining and discussing the appropriateness of use). One of the most rewarding experiences for learners is to use digital cameras to capture their own perspective of the environment – a child's eye view of the world around them ('These are the toilets. This is the teacher. We use the computer for learning. We hang our clothes on these pegs to keep them safe.') This is an invaluable experience that allows learners to gain ownership of the class and to develop a sense of understanding of the world. It's true that this can be done without using digital cameras, but their use enriches the experience and provides a reference that can be stored, analysed and shared.

ICT can enrich the early years classroom

Tools

- Book or PowerPoint version of the nursery rhyme or story.
- Mobile phone to contact the character.
- Voice recorder to record what the characters might be saying or thinking.
- Digital camera for taking images of the pupils as the characters or for them to take photos of certain scenarios in the story.

- Teach the pupils how to use the equipment, such as how to take a picture or what to press to record sound.

- Leave the equipment around the class whenever and wherever possible, as this gives learners opportunities to explore and practise their skills.

- Provide meaningful opportunities for learners to use their skills. Display a list of nursery rhyme characters and their mobile phone numbers so that they can use the phones to call them.

- Whenever possible, invite parents and carers to participate when using the technology to allow skills to be shared. Share outcomes with an audience – not necessarily an outside one.

- Role play is key! Allow children to role-play with ICT in the environment – this can include items such as parking meters, automatic doors, televisions, microwave ovens, fridges, home phones, video recorders, bedside clocks and alarms.

Further activities

▌Movie making with early years

The early years classroom and movie making were made for each other. Role-play activities in a classroom are natural narrative forms that would be at home on film to watch, enjoy and revise. There are obvious benefits to recording children performing and using this with them.

There are also many benefits with using film and allowing learners to become the movie makers. Much like the use of digital cameras, movie cameras can be used to capture the moment and elaborate on understanding.

Children could use a movie camera to record mini-beasts in the environment while the technology captures what they are saying. This idea is powerful and useful as it can be instantaneous and things can be captured that may otherwise be missed. Often only a few minutes of filming are needed – both of the children and by the children – to support the objectives or purpose of the activity.

Using a video camera

Asking children to record each other is a valuable social experience and when played on a big screen it has a 'wow' factor that can be difficult to replicate. Many applications, such as Windows Movie Maker, are easy for children to use.

Alternatively, the software that comes with many cameras allows pupils to make decisions about the footage. Movie making can also be used to bring story-telling to life as children can re-create a famous story or retell one of their own. They can also recount dreams and ideas and have these captured on film and played back.

A permanent camera could be set up, say in the wet play area, to allow learners to take on a certain role if they know they are playing for a camera. This helps to develop their imaginative thinking and exploration of characters. Learners using cameras to capture certain situations in the classroom, such as tension and arguments, allows individuals or the whole class to discuss the PSHE elements, considering which choices are being made and actions taken.

Movie making is a great way to share information between the school and the community. If your school has a website, movies can be uploaded and circulated. If there are issues with using images of children, showing films made by children (rather than of children) gets over this. If the movies are shared at the end of the day or during the week, parents who do not have computers are able to participate too.

Sharing movies

▌Programmable toys

Making your classroom ICT-rich by using programmable toys that children can understand and respond to makes the use of toys in the classroom fun, engaging and valuable. Programmable robots encourage the development of higher-order thinking skills and a deeper understanding of 'If I do this, this happens. What happens if I do this?' or 'How do I make it do this?'. Learners can also explore the possibilities and limitations of what the toys can do. Problem solving with programmable toys is a great way of getting pupils to develop their vocabulary (directional, mathematical or whatever context the problem is set in) and explore what is and what is not possible.

Using a simple program acts as a good introduction to directional problem-solving activities. Questions can be introduced, such as 'How do we get the car from the church to the school?' and 'Where is the hospital?'. This activity can be translated using maps, digital images and programmable toys such as Roamers. Using maps of the local area and digital images of places that the children recognize makes the activity 'real' and pupils can discuss experiences that are real to them, such as routes they may take and things that they may see.

Pupils can also explore what happens with different sets of programming, such as 'What will happen if...?'. Lego Mindstorms Robolab allows learners to use light sensors and different materials. They can be shown how to take a light reading of the classroom. Pupils can use this information to decide which material is best to make windows for a dolls' house. They can place the sensor against different types of material, such as light, dark, translucent and opaque and then, with adult support, use the light reading to decide if the material is suitable or not. Learners don't need to be able to do this independently and should not be expected to. This activity works best if they work in small groups with adult support or as a whole class with the teacher. It is how the technology is used that is important not the use of the technology.

Using a programmable toy

Top tips

Early years

➡ An ICT corner (where the computer might be) is a good idea for teaching ICT skills. However, incorporating ICT into all areas is essential to allow pupils to explore and investigate potential uses.

➡ Incorporate the use of ICT in imaginative ways, such as by using underwater webcams to reinforce the idea of 'under the sea' or a movie to show what different workers do.

➡ Some toys are ICT-rich and can be used to encourage development. Robosapien, sound recorders and remote control toys are some of the best.

➡ Digital cameras, movie recorders and sound recorders give learners an unconventional means of recording. Using these methods to record is a great equalizer and allows their understanding to be captured.

➡ Introduce mock-ICT set-ups where actual ICT is not available, such as washing machines, parking meters and so on. These can be re-created using cardboard, paint and digital images.

➡ Let pupils lead and explore the technology. It's important for them to be shown how to use equipment correctly, but it is also important to allow them to 'play' with the equipment and develop their own understanding.

➡ ICT is fun! It doesn't always work, but when it does it's fantastic and can bring experiences to life. Involve children in the process of choosing when to use it and when not to use it. When it doesn't work, go to plan B!

- If you don't have the budget for a class set of specialist primary-level video cameras, think about using cheap pre-paid 3G mobile phones (with the SIM card disabled) in combination with free video-editing software such as Windows Movie Maker.

- Display board activities are incredible fun. Using 3G mobile phones in combination with a portable photo printer enables every activity to result in a colourful and creative record celebrating the activity and the learners' achievements.

Postscript

We have written this book to help you make creative use of ICT a regular part of your 'real teaching' rather than something fun you do when everything else is up to date. We hope we have managed to inspire you to have a go.

We have tried to make the range of ideas for activities generic enough to illustrate wider points and specific enough to let you get started with something to base activities on right away.

There is one thing we haven't covered that we would like to share now. There is a risk in the creative classroom that you will inadvertently make illegal use of somebody else's intellectual property. It happens – you need a picture of a sunflower for that excellent piece of drama, and a short trip to Google later and you have used somebody else's work without their permission. Another risk is that in sharing your work you may lead somebody else into the same situation. We would like to end this book by doing something practical: explaining what are the limits of your freedom to create and how to protect that creative work.

What can you use?

WEBSITE

The guiding principle is called fair dealing and if you want to read more about this topic try searching on Google (www.google.co.uk) and seeing where it takes you.

There is a difference between producing something for you or your employer and producing something as part of learning (whether it be making class material or a learner carrying out a task).

If a piece of work isn't directly related to pupils' learning, you should be using material that belongs only to you or your institution, or that is copyright free. If something says 'reproduce with the author's permission' then that's what you should do. This is important for two reasons:

- ➡ we are educators so we have to set an example;
- ➡ we are good educators and so should not lose our job (or worse) by being prosecuted by an irate copyright holder.

It's easy to think 'Who will know and who will care?' but there are two answers to that question. First, learners will know and they will mimic your behaviour. Second, you don't know who will find out – one unfortunate soul merrily photocopied huge tracts from a textbook and sent them home with his class, only to discover that one of the parents was employed by the publisher...

If it's for the purpose of learning, you have a considerable degree of freedom to use material from any source. However, do make sure it's properly credited and make that a part of the learning activity. Be careful if the product of this use is then used again elsewhere. A good example of this would be if a learner used some images from the internet in a presentation made in class. Let's say someone from the education authority saw it, thought it was excellent and made it part of a pack for teachers. Those images may then have been used illegally.

The key questions to ask are:

➡ Will it be used only for non-profit making educational use?

➡ Will this be the first use of this material? If the material is available on the web or in print you are OK here, but fair dealing isn't usually available for unpublished material unless such material has been made generally available.

➡ Are you using a snippet of a piece of work or reproducing it lock, stock and barrel? Taking a small section of text from an article is different to using the whole thing as if it were yours.

➡ Does your use of this material lower its value in any way? You could argue, for example, that a student taking a clip from a movie as part of an analysis of the film would be OK, but if they were to reproduce the key final scene and publish it on the internet that would reduce the value of that film as a whole in the market and so be unfair.

Using small parts of material from the web for learning – where it isn't published beyond the classroom itself – is generally accepted as fair.

Those who are perhaps most upset by software piracy are programmers. Those who are perhaps the keenest on legal music downloads are musicians. If we want learners to care about respecting the value of other people's work, we need to make them the owners of their own.

Who can use your work?

Your pupils should consider who owns their work – both morally and legally. We suggest you first speak to your headteacher to see if there is a policy that binds you and your class. Pupils need to be aware of the following issues:

➡ Who owns their work?

➡ Do they own their own movies, songs and text or do you? For example, if an outside consultant wanted to use a film made by your class, who decides if that is OK? By respecting the ownership of your learners' intellectual property you will be teaching them about the (market) value of thought.

WEBSITE

A great resource for this is the Creative Commons website at creativecommons.org, which includes a number of example licence agreements in everyday language you could agree with your class and post somewhere suitable.

Acknowledgements

With thanks to the following for permission to reproduce screenshots in this book:

Apple: pages 116 (top), 146, 147, 148 and 150 (bottom)

Audacity Developer Team: pages 37, 78 (bottom), 94 and 95 (both)

BBC Motion Gallery: page 91

British Pathe: page 88 (both)

Coding Monkeys: page 28

Google: page 100 (both)

Immersive Education: pages 17 and 118 (bottom)

Microsoft product screenshots reprinted with permission from Microsoft Corporation

Screenshot reproduced with permission from Multimap, Getmapping, Tele Atlas NV and Ordnance Survey: pages 42 (both) and 43

O_2: page 144

Ohio State University: page 118 (top)

plasq: page 29, made with Comic Life plasq.com

RemotePC: page 133

Sibelius: page 117

With thanks to the pupils, parents and teachers at the following schools for permission to reproduce photographs in this book:

Campion School

Delapre Primary School

Latimer Community Arts College

Lyncrest Primary School

Lumbertubs Primary School

Hardingstone Primary School

Nassington School

Rectory Farm Primary School

Simon de Senlis Primary School

St Luke's CE Primary School

Weavers School

Wilbarston CE Primary School

Every effort has been made to contact copyright holders of material reproduced in this book. The publishers apologize for any omissions and will be pleased to rectify them at the earliest opportunity.

Index

Other titles from Network Continuum Education

ACCELERATED LEARNING SERIES

Accelerated Learning: A User's Guide by Alistair Smith, Mark Lovatt & Derek Wise
Accelerated Learning in the Classroom by Alistair Smith
Accelerated Learning in Practice by Alistair Smith
The ALPS Approach: Accelerated learning in primary schools by Alistair Smith & Nicola Call
The ALPS Approach Resource Book by Alistair Smith & Nicola Call
MapWise by Oliver Caviglioli & Ian Harris
Creating an Accelerated Learning School by Mark Lovatt & Derek Wise
Thinking for Learning by Mel Rockett & Simon Percival
Reaching out to all learners by Cheshire LEA
Move It: Physical movement and learning by Alistair Smith
Coaching Solutions by Will Thomas & Alistair Smith
Coaching Solutions Resource Book by Will Thomas

ABLE AND TALENTED CHILDREN COLLECTION

Effective Provision for Able and Talented Children by Barry Teare
Effective Resources for Able and Talented Children by Barry Teare
More Effective Resources for Able and Talented Children by Barry Teare
Challenging Resources for Able and Talented Children by Barry Teare
Enrichment Activities for Able and Talented Children by Barry Teare
Parents' and Carers' Guide for Able and Talented Children by Barry Teare

LEARNING TO LEARN

The Practical Guide to Revision Techniques by Simon Percival
Let's Learn How to Learn: Workshops for Key Stage 2 by UFA National Team
Brain Friendly Revision by UFA National Team
Learning to Learn for Life: Research and practical examples for Foundation Stage and Key Stage 1
    by Rebecca Goodbourn, Susie Parsons, Julia Wright, Steve Higgins & Kate Wall
Creating a Learning to Learn School by Toby Greany & Jill Rodd
Teaching Pupils How to Learn by Bill Lucas, Toby Greany, Jill Rodd & Ray Wicks

EXCITING ICT

New Tools for Learning: Accelerated learning meets ICT by John Davitt
Exciting ICT in Maths by Alison Clark-Jeavons
Exciting ICT in English by Tony Archdeacon
Exciting ICT in History by Ben Walsh

PRIMARY RESOURCES

Foundations of Literacy by Sue Palmer & Ros Bayley
Flying Start with Literacy by Ros Bayley
The Thinking Child by Nicola Call with Sally Featherstone
The Thinking Child Resource Book by Nicola Call with Sally Featherstone
Critical Skills in the Early Years by Vicki Charlesworth
Towards Successful Learning by Diana Pardoe
But Why? Developing philosophical thinking in the classroom by Sara Stanley with Steve Bowkett

Help Your Child To Succeed by Bill Lucas & Alistair Smith
Help Your Child To Succeed – Toolkit by Bill Lucas & Alistair Smith
Promoting Children's Well-Being in the Primary Years:
    The Right from the Start handbook edited by Andrew Burrell & Jeni Riley
Numeracy Activities Key Stage 2 by Afzal Ahmed & Honor Williams
Numeracy Activities Key Stage 3 by Afzal Ahmed, Honor Williams & George Wickham

LEARNING THROUGH SONGS

That's English! Learning English through songs (Key Stage 2) by Tim Harding
That's Maths! Learning maths through songs (Key Stage 2) by Tim Harding
Maths in Action! Learning maths through music & animation – interactive CD-ROM
    (Key Stage 2) by Tim Harding
That's Science! Learning science through songs (Key Stage 2) by Tim Harding
This is Science! Learning science through songs and stories (Key Stage 1) by Tim Harding

VISUAL LEARNING

Seeing History: Visual learning strategies & resources for Key Stage 3 by Tom Haward
Reaching out to all thinkers by Ian Harris & Oliver Caviglioli
Think it–Map it! by Ian Harris & Oliver Caviglioli
Thinking Skills & Eye Q by Oliver Caviglioli, Ian Harris & Bill Tindall

DISPLAY MATERIAL

Bright Sparks by Alistair Smith
More Bright Sparks by Alistair Smith
Leading Learning by Alistair Smith
Move It Posters: Physical movement and learning by Alistair Smith
Multiple Intelligence Posters (KS1 and KS2–4) edited by Alistair Smith
Emotional Intelligence Posters (KS1 and KS2–4) edited by Alistair Smith
Thinking Skills & Eye Q Posters by Oliver Caviglioli, Ian Harris & Bill Tindall

EMOTIONAL INTELLIGENCE

Multiple Intelligences in Practice: Enhancing self-esteem and learning in the classroom
    by Mike Fleetham
Moving to Secondary School by Lynda Measor with Mike Fleetham
Future Directions by Diane Carrington & Helen Whitten
Tooncards: A multi-purpose resource for developing communication skills by Chris Terrell
Becoming Emotionally Intelligent by Catherine Corrie
Lend Us Your Ears by Rosemary Sage
Class Talk by Rosemary Sage
A World of Difference by Rosemary Sage
Best behaviour and Best behaviour FIRST AID
    by Peter Relf, Rod Hirst, Jan Richardson & Georgina Youdell
    Best behaviour FIRST AID also available separately
Self-Intelligence by Stephen Bowkett
Imagine That... by Stephen Bowkett
ALPS StoryMaker by Stephen Bowkett
StoryMaker Catch Pack by Stephen Bowkett
With Drama in Mind by Patrice Baldwin

PERSONALIZING LEARNING

Personalizing Learning: Transforming education for every child
by John West-Burnham & Max Coates

Transforming Education for Every Child: A practical handbook
by John West-Burnham & Max Coates

Personalizing Learning in the 21st Century edited by Sara de Freitas & Chris Yapp

The Power of Diversity by Barbara Prashnig

Learning Styles in Action by Barbara Prashnig

EFFECTIVE LEARNING & LEADERSHIP

Effective Heads of Department by Phil Jones & Nick Sparks

Leading the Learning School by Colin Weatherley

Transforming Teaching & Learning by Colin Weatherley with Bruce Bonney, John Kerr & Jo Morrison

Classroom Management by Philip Waterhouse & Chris Dickinson

Effective Learning Activities by Chris Dickinson

Making Pupil Data Powerful by Maggie Pringle & Tony Cobb

Raising Boys' Achievement by Jon Pickering

Getting Started by Henry Liebling

Closing the Learning Gap by Mike Hughes

Strategies for Closing the Learning Gap by Mike Hughes with Andy Vass

Tweak to Transform by Mike Hughes

Lessons are for Learning by Mike Hughes

Nurturing Independent Thinkers edited by Mike Bosher & Patrick Hazlewood

Effective Teachers by Tony Swainston

Effective Teachers in Primary Schools by Tony Swainston

Effective Leadership in Schools by Tony Swainston

Leading Change in Schools: A Practical Handbook by Sian Case

VISIONS OF EDUCATION SERIES

Discover Your Hidden Talents: The essential guide to lifelong learning by Bill Lucas

The Brain's Behind It by Alistair Smith

Wise Up by Guy Claxton

The Unfinished Revolution by John Abbott & Terry Ryan

The Learning Revolution by Gordon Dryden & Jeannette Vos

SCHOOL GOVERNORS

Questions School Governors Ask by Joan Sallis

Basics for School Governors by Joan Sallis

The Effective School Governor by David Marriott (including audio tape)

For more information and ordering details, please consult our website www.networkcontinuum.co.uk

Network Continuum Education – much more than publishing...

Network Continuum Education Conferences – Invigorate your teaching

Each term NCE runs a wide range of conferences on cutting edge issues in teaching and learning at venues around the UK. The emphasis is always highly practical. Regular presenters include some of our top-selling authors such as Sue Palmer, Mike Hughes and Steve Bowkett. Dates and venues for our current programme of conferences can be found on our website www.networkcontinuum.co.uk.

NCE online Learning Style Analysis – Find out how your students prefer to learn

Discovering what makes your students tick is the key to personalizing learning. NCE's Learning Style Analysis is a 50-question online evaluation that can give an immediate and thorough learning profile for every student in your class. It reveals how, when and where they learn best, whether they are right brain or left brain dominant, analytic or holistic, whether they are strongly auditory, visual, kinesthetic or tactile... and a great deal more. And for teachers who'd like to take the next step, LSA enables you to create a whole-class profile for precision lesson planning.

Developed by The Creative Learning Company in New Zealand and based on the work of Learning Styles expert Barbara Prashnig, this powerful tool allows you to analyse your own and your students' learning preferences in a more detailed way than any other product we have ever seen. To find out more about Learning Style Analysis or to order profiles visit www.networkcontinuum.co.uk/lsa.

Also available: Teaching Style Analysis and Working Style Analysis.

NCE's Critical Skills Programme – Teach your students skills for lifelong learning

The Critical Skills Programme puts pupils at the heart of learning, by providing the skills required to be successful in school and life. Classrooms are developed into effective learning environments, where pupils work collaboratively and feel safe enough to take 'learning risks'. Pupils have more ownership of their learning across the whole curriculum and are encouraged to develop not only subject knowledge but the fundamental skills of:

- problem solving
- creative thinking
- decision making
- communication
- management
- organization

- leadership
- self-direction
- quality working
- collaboration
- enterprise
- community involvement

'The Critical Skills Programme... energizes students to think in an enterprising way. CSP gets students to think for themselves, solve problems in teams, think outside the box, to work in a structured manner. CSP is the ideal way to forge an enterprising student culture.'

Rick Lee, Deputy Director, Barrow Community Learning Partnership

To find out more about CSP training visit the Critical Skills Programme website at www.criticalskills.co.uk